Séance Experiments

Séance Experiments

By

Kalila Smith
and
Sid Patrick

Séance Experiments

Copyright © 2016 Kalila Smith and Sid Patrick

Cover design by Lori Osif
Image by Elena Niccolai via Dreamstime.com

All rights reserved. No part of this book may be reproduced, duplicated, copied, or transmitted in any form or by any means without the express written consent and permission of the author and publisher.

This is a work of memory and storytelling. The names, characters, places, and incidents are known publicly, are common knowledge, or are used only from a memoir point of view. All opinions and events related are told from the author's point of view. For entertainment purposes only.

Published by
Dark Oak Press
Kerlak Enterprises, Inc.
Memphis, TN
www.darkoakpress.com

Trade Paperback
ISBN 13: 978-1-941754-66-5
Library of Congress Control Number: 2016955097
First Printing: 2016

This book is printed on acid free paper.

Printed in the United States of America

Dedicated to the spirits of our loved ones without whom, this journey would not be possible.

Acknowledgments

Our sincere gratitude goes to everyone who shared their personal experiences from the Séance Room. Special thanks go to Billy Roberts, Dr. Charlotte Pipes, Dr. Fayr Barkley, Denise Baudier, Silvia Santos, Sonnet Ireland, Susan Moody, Patricia Lund, Patricia Levie, and Heather Monell for their assistance in this project. We send out a special thank you to Dr. Andrew Ward for his editing expertise. We also offer a huge thank you to everyone at Dark Oak Media and Press for their continued support and assistance.

We thank all of the spirits who assisted us in these experiments and continue to guide us in our spiritual work.

Table of Contents

Foreword by Billy Roberts i
Preface 1
Chapter One - The Medium 9
Chapter Two - Becoming the Tube 17
Chapter Three - The Circle 29
Chapter Four - Getting Physical 39
Chapter Five - Birth of the Séance Room 49
Chapter Six - Written in the Stars 59
Chapter Seven - Altered States 67
Chapter Eight - Walkers between Worlds 77
Chapter Nine - The Healers 85
Chapter Ten – Entranced 93
Chapter Eleven - Back to the Table 101
Chapter Twelve - Sacred Journeys 113
Chapter Thirteen - Mysteries Revealed 119
Chapter Fourteen - Hidden Dangers 129
Chapter Fifteen - The Unwelcome Visitor 139
Chapter Sixteen - Lifting the Veil 149
Chapter Seventeen - Science Validates Spirit 159
Chapter Eighteen - Your Own Séance Experiments 167
Chapter Nineteen - Adventures in the Cabinet 173
Chapter Twenty - The Power of Spirit 181
Final Thoughts 187
Glossary 191

Foreword

I first met Kalila Smith in 2003 when we worked together on a documentary to promote Sony's Playstation 2 Game Ghost Hunter, filmed on location in New Orleans and surrounding areas. We have kept in touch from that moment on and have since worked together in the UK in 2014. Although when I met Kalila she was already a well-established and respected exponent of the paranormal, it is my opinion that her true spiritual journey really began with the untimely passing of her daughter, Stephanie. As is very often the case, the loss of a loved one, particularly a son or daughter, takes a person to a very different spiritual level, and Kalila was certainly no exception, why should she be? Losing a child can very often cause a person to completely turn away from all things spiritual; however, this was definitely not the case where Kalila was concerned. I can see from reading this book just how deeply she was affected by the loss of Stephanie, and how determined she actually was to maintain a 'connection' with the daughter she had loved and lost. In fact, motivated by her daughter's passing, this book clearly highlights her journey even further into the world of the paranormal. Helped and encouraged by her good friend and fellow New Orleans medium, Sid Patrick, Kalila began to develop and cultivate her own mediumistic skills, and to maintain that all-important connection she had always had with her now deceased daughter. In this book Kalila makes a detailed study of various types of paranormal phenomena, from table tipping to different aspects of physical mediumship. The more Kalila discovered in the vast world of the paranormal, the more her own mediumistic skills began to unfold. As far as I am concerned, this book explores the other side of Kalila Smith's personality, her beliefs, and how she has dealt with her deep sadness caused by the loss of her daughter. But, more importantly to me, she reveals her analytical eye and her ability to discern the spirits. She clearly has a no-nonsense way sorting out the wheat from the chaff and with an ability to discriminate between genuine mediums and those unscrupulous people who simply exploit the vulnerability of the bereaved.

As well as revealing Kalila's personal quest into the world of the paranormal, this book is an insight into a subject that has become extremely fashionable over the last ten years or so. It also makes a detailed analysis of the various messages Kalila has received from her daughter through different mediums, and how Stephanie confirmed to her mother that reincarnation is a fact. The way in which Kalila approaches the subject matter contained in her book gives it a very broad appeal, and whether you are actually involved in the paranormal, or simply have a superficial interest in it, she more or less covers every aspect of the subject in these pages. She relates her experiences with ectoplasm, trance and channeling, table tipping and even the phenomena that occur during the Spiritualist séance. Kalila explores the nature of communication with the 'spirit world', and even takes a brief sojourn into the world of Aleister Crowley, the infamous high ceremonial magician who died in veritable poverty, and who is today revered as the Master of the Golden Dawn. In her book, Kalila Smith most certainly has a voice that clearly sets her apart from other mediums and paranormal investigators, showing that her expertise is not confined to the parameters of 'ghost hunting', and that she has a wealth of knowledge that covers almost every area of the world of mediums and the paranormal.

As well as her own experiences with mediums and the paranormal, she also relates some anecdotal accounts of other peoples' involvements with the subject, offering some very important and sound advice of the things to do as opposed to the things not to do. Having been brought up in a family of mediums in Liverpool, England, I have met and worked with some of the greatest exponents of mediumship over the last 35 years or so, and I can honestly affirm that Kalila Smith is already emerging as a worthy ambassador for Spiritualism and the paranormal, not just in the USA, but in the UK and many other countries. She is an eloquent speaker with an inimitable modern mediumistic style that stands out from others I have seen, either in the United Kingdom or the USA. Her knowledge comes across in everything she writes, and I know this book will satisfy all the readers' paranormal needs.

I am always reminded of the ancient precept, 'The thousand mile journey begins with the single step.' In my opinion, Kalila Smith has taken much more than that single step; and although there are many rocky roads to travel, she can rest assured that her daughter, Stephanie, will always be by her side.

Billy Roberts, Psychic/Medium: Cornwall, England

Preface
(Kalila Smith)

I still remember it as if it was yesterday, that first reading from a medium. It was several months after my daughter had died. Little did I know at the time, what doors would open because of it.

I was in a great deal of pain. I spent every day of the first few months buried in my writing. I completed two books in a matter of weeks. After that, I found myself alone in my new life. I had received many comforting After Death Communications (ADCs) from her but they were neither continual nor was it consistent. I was convinced that she could communicate with me, but it was not the same as having her with me on a daily basis. I could not hug or laugh with her, or take her to a movie. As comforting as her ADCs were I still missed her desperately.

I knew that she wanted me to evolve spiritually. I also knew that for whatever reasons unbeknownst to me, her time here was done. Mine was not. I had to somehow find my place in this world again. I did not know what or where I wanted to be. Did it matter anyway? What I wanted was not possible. As I had done so many times before in my life, I settled. The problem was that this time I was not sure for what exactly I was settling. I had not asked for my life to take this turn for the worse. The last time I planned anything it was to take my daughter to a wrestling match after she recovered from surgery. She never did.

I became obsessed with what lies beyond this physical plane of existence, if anything at all. My only goal was to occupy my time. I managed to keep myself busy in order to avoid the pain of my loss. If not, I would drown in my grief. For the sake of my other daughter and granddaughters, I had to pull myself together. I needed to move forward. For the sake of my daughter who had crossed over, I had to do whatever it took to make sure that I would reunite with her when it was my time to leave this world.

One evening, I rushed to work through the streets of the French Quarter as I had for many years. I had not been able to decide whether I would drive the following morning to a sci-fi/paranormal convention in another state or spend the weekend home. Normally, such a decision would not be a difficult task but it had only been a few months since Stephanie's death. My mind was jumbled from the fog of grief. Making even the smallest decision had become a chore for me. Even if I did make one, I would often become hesitant and change my mind. Everything was scrambled for me. Just waking up in the morning and going about my usual routine was a major undertaking.

As I stepped up onto the curb on the corner, an acquaintance of mine was exiting the supermarket. During a brief conversation, he handed me a business card. It belonged to a medium, Sid Patrick, who held a monthly metaphysical fair in a nearby suburb. I realized immediately that I needed to attend this event. I had been in a very bad mental state, practically on the verge of a breakdown. I suffered from extreme muscle tension and pain. I had knots in every part of my body. Everything hurt. I had gained forty pounds since my daughter's death. Due to a degenerated disc in my lower back, I could barely stand up straight. I was exhausted all the time, yet, could not sleep at night. I had hoped that by seeing a medium, I could find some solace. The following day, I attended the event. After checking out all I could about this medium, I scheduled a private mediumship session. When I arrived for my session, I was escorted to a parlor area to wait for him. I fought to hold back the tears of desperation. I could hear him in the other room with another customer. She was yelling at him for getting nothing.

"Great," I thought.

Sid Patrick came into the room and introduced himself to me. He apologized for the client before explaining that not everyone is always able to connect. He then offered the reading at no charge if he did not get anything. He also explained that the other client was late and then pressed him for time, putting a great deal of pressure on the session. I followed him into the other room to begin the session.

Immediately, Sid got a vision. He said he felt sadness. He felt that there was something that I had not resolved yet. He also indicated that he saw a young girl.

He asked, "Is this your daughter?"

I took a deep breath trying not to lose my composure and answered, "Yes, it is."

He then asked, "Is your daughter still with us…here?"

"No, she is not," I answered choking back my tears.

"I was hoping that was not the case," he said.

He continued, "She is here….no wait… there is also someone else. There is a male and a female. They're both coming at me. They travel together."

This was not the first confirmation that Stephanie was with a close friend on the other side. Finally, I relaxed. I settled into the chair. I went from complete loss of belief to believer because I knew that he was seeing her. I listened as Sid described what was going on beyond the veil.

Sid paced back and forth as he gave me a vivid description of my friend. I sat quietly answering "yes," as he asked questions relating to identifying him.

He told me that my friend was very protective of Stephanie. "Oh, she's saying a bit too over protective," he added.

Sid gave accurate details on messages that could only come from this particular person. Sid then asked my friend to step back to allow Stephanie to speak for herself.

Sid told me, "She's saying 'I want to talk to my mother for one minute. Mom, you know I'm with you,' the little clues that you get are coming from me."

Sid said, "She is saying, 'Mom, you were the most positive thing in my life."

I completely broke down listening to her message to me. It was a relief to know that she was reaching out to me from the other side.

Sid continued, "She's saying that she chose you as her mother. She thanks you for all you gave her. You gave her opportunities that so many mothers might not have. She is thanking you for letting her get involved in life. She wants to tell you that she is okay. She knows that you constantly worried about her. She says, *Mom, I'm just a shout away.*"

Sid went on, "She's fine. She wants you to be able to move on but not forget her. She wants you to release the emotions then she will be able to get closer to you."

He described our connection to the spirit world like a big piece of cellophane that is stretched across the two worlds, dividing them. They can see and hear us. We cannot always see and hear them. They try to push through that cellophane to reach you.

"Imagine how frustrating it is for spirits when they are trying to communicate," he told me.

"She does come through but she feels like you don't pay attention. So I need you to pay attention," he said.

She told Sid that she is with me all the time. He related, "She feels that she is still here just as she was always still on the other side a great deal. She always walked in both worlds. She still does."

When I left the session, a large crow perched himself on the front porch of the home where Sid was reading. It stayed for several hours. Sid felt certain that the crow was for me. Several days after the reading, a beautiful Monarch butterfly appeared in my driveway. It flew over my car. From that moment forward, I received visits from butterflies on a daily basis. Sometimes it was a large Monarch, sometimes it was a black one with blue markings, often both. They appeared regardless of where I was.

Shortly after her death, I received a card in the mail from the mother of one of Stephanie's friends. Stephanie had known Troy since they were in kindergarten. They were life-long friends who seemed to be connected even when they were apart. She wanted to make me aware that she believed her son had received communication from Stephanie. He kept showing her our phone number written on a piece of paper and repeated, "my friend," over and over to her. After I read the note, I left my home to make my way to work. Tears streamed down my face. I sobbed as I drove around the block. I became aware of a large butterfly flying alongside my car. I immediately felt relief, knowing that she was with me.

The butterfly visits became a daily treat for me. I did not merely see them in the distance but rather they flew to me. One afternoon, as I stood in my backyard, a huge Monarch flew over my shoulder brushing against my hair. It flew right up in a figure eight pattern in my face then darted off into the trees. On another day, I saw one fly above me at my older daughter's house. That same day, I decided to see a doctor for a bronchitis attack. What appeared to be that same butterfly flew in a figure eight pattern outside the glass door of the doctor's office. Throughout the summer, butterflies appeared and followed me everywhere I went. When the butterflies were no longer in season she used other insects.

Then one night, Stephanie finally appeared in a dream. She seemed to be veiled behind some sort of sheer, misty partition. Only her hands could be seen clearly. She tapped her index fingers together lining them up. She made the shape of a heart with her fingers. I said to her, "I love you, too, baby girl."

She then put one hand over the other and crossed her thumbs waving her hands like butterfly wings. I remembered something that I had forgotten a long time ago. When she was a toddler, she learned sign language. She often made this sign to symbolize a butterfly when she was a small child. Clearly, seeing this in the dream was validation that the butterflies were coming from her. Sid was right. When I was ready to receive the gift of her communication I did, with clarity.

The ADCs continued to stream. Not only butterflies, but beautiful flowers appeared out of nowhere. A beautiful red flower had appeared along the fence in my backyard. Unfortunately, the lawn crew accidently cut it down while trimming the lawn. On the fourth of July, I noticed that although it had been three weeks since the flower had been destroyed, a single petal was on the ground where it once grew. It was as fresh as a live flower but in the shape of a heart. A couple of months later, on my oldest daughter's birthday, several red flowers grew overnight out in the middle of her yard. No one had planted them. These were gifts sent to us from Stephanie.

Heart-shaped flower found in garden.

Months later, when I went for my annual doctor's visit, I received a strange message from the nurse on duty. She weighed me and asked how I had been feeling. I told her that I had just lost my daughter a few months earlier, hence the substantial weight gain. She gazed off for a second then shivered. "I just got a chill," she said.

Then she went on, "Your daughter is still with you, she's right next to you. She says that she is happy now, and in a better place. She says that God called her home." Then she shivered again. She ran her hand over her arm, "I got a chill right here," she said.

As I was leaving, the nurse smiled at me and said, "Your angel is right beside you."

I am eternally grateful to Sid for opening up the door of communication with my daughter. I began to attend classes at his center and signed up for his intense mediumship development courses. I was determined to fine tune my own medium skills in order to keep in close communication with my daughter.

So began a journey not only for me but for Sid Patrick and all of the others who became a part of the experiments in the séance room. This book is a record of our experiences as we further developed our relationship with Spirit*.

Séance Experiments

The accounts written herein are actual experiences as they are recalled by those who experienced them. The idea of turning these experiences into a book was a secondary thought. The spiritual journey that became this book began only as experiments for all of us. None of us embarked on this journey with any agendas. We did what felt natural.

The spirits who assisted with these experiments played an important role in bringing people together. Certain people crossed each other's paths at specific times. Groups were brought together for specific messages. Without a doubt, there was a plan somewhere in place, although it was unknown to us at the time. We were drawn towards certain circumstances. In the end we realized that there were no accidents or coincidences.

As we documented the experiments, we kept them as true as possible although in many instances, names were changed to protect anonymity.

For the purpose of understanding how the process of physical mediumship works, one must first understand what brought us to this level in the first place. Although the first couple of chapters may seem a bit dry at first to the reader, the information will be useful later when the focus is more on actual Spirit activity. It becomes clear how Spirit aligned things all along.

*When describing Spirit in the sense of referring to the collective consciousness of the Divine, (God), the word is capitalized.

Chapter One
The Medium

From the time he was a small child, Sid Patrick knew that he was no ordinary person. Like so many who have communicated with spirits, he grew up assuming it was a normal part of who he was. He never questioned it. Like many others, he found himself caught up in simply living life. He was born to help others, bringing messages of hope to those in pain. Nothing in his life was a coincidence. His entire journey has been a series of serendipitous adventures that brought him to where he is today.

He told me the story of his childhood:

Many years ago, as long as I can remember, my Aunt Ethel, my maternal grandmother's sister, read playing cards for her friends. She wouldn't read for the family except for one particular aunt. She didn't want to know certain things about family so she would not read them. She was very accurate.

I do remember as I go back even younger, when I was about two or three years old, we rented a very old two-story apartment above a garage. I can remember the old time bathtub. The floors were very distinct in that they were very old wood floors. You could see in between the slats down into the garage below. My parents slept in the living area. My sister and I shared the bedroom. There was a lot next door to this place that we rented.

I remember going on these journeys, where I would visit this man. He had white hair and a white beard. I later learned that he was one of my guides. The memories are very sharp. I remember him serving me toast with maple syrup and milk. His house was one big room, very open. The whole scene reminded me of the old Shirley Temple movie, Heidi; the grandfather's house. The kitchen was antiquated with a large wood burning stove. On top of it was an old drip coffee pot. He did have a toaster, though. We would sit and talk about life in general. I journeyed to see him at least once a month. I walked across the lot on those days and went into his house. But other days, the house wasn't there. Now that I'm older, I relate to him. I know who he is but then I had no idea. He's been with me that long. I remember him at that very young age showing me things. He talked some but he did more by showing me things like places I would go or things that I would do. I remember him showing me Egypt. I haven't gotten there yet, but I've gotten to Africa. I remember him showing me pyramids. I can smell the coffee and the maple syrup to this day. He would give me black licorice and I would take it home. I have lots of connections with licorice now. He was a wonderful person that would never do anything wrong. It's as clear as a bell.

Another entity that I encountered at a young age was a little red-haired boy. He often played hide and seek with me. It was usually at night when I was ready to go to sleep. He would peek around a corner then duck and hide. He would stick his head from around the corner then move away giggling. I later learned at a spiritual camp that this little boy was my doorkeeper. A doorkeeper, sometimes referred to as gatekeeper, is one who brings spirits in for communication. They open the doors for communication between our world and the worlds of spirits. This little boy remained my doorkeeper until my mother's death. Now she is my doorkeeper. When I do a reading, I give my mother a sign and ask her to bring the spirits in. When I take my wedding ring off, my mother knows that I am ready to work.

She guards that door for me. She protects me to keep love and light and only good things coming through. We pray to Archangel Michael for protection then she opens the door.

The lady who raised me came from the Louisiana/Arkansas line. She told me ghost stories growing up. She took me to the place where she had grown up. I spent a summer there with her when I was nine years old. She showed me haunted places in her home town. We shared many stories about our experiences.

Chapter One: The Medium

Sid's aunt taught his older sister how to read playing cards. His younger sister had the gift of prophetic dreams. But neither of them went down the same path as he. He began to read cards at age thirteen. Then as a young teen he pushed away from the metaphysical focusing on school and social activities. He admitted fighting against some of his intuitiveness. Fascinated by healing, he enrolled in nursing school. A guidance counselor urged him to change his major to embalming. At the time he did not realize that it was Spirit directing him. The suggestion felt right for him so he followed it. Oddly enough, once he had completed his courses and began working in a funeral home, many of his relatives died one right after another.

As an embalmer, he found that his greatest talent was as a restorative artist. He was able to restore badly decomposed or damaged bodies from accidents so that their loved ones could see them. He used various make-up effects to rebuild tissue around the eyes if they were sunk in, bringing back their natural look. It was in this line of work that Sid learned about grief and how to help others handle the loss of a loved one. The experience humbled him, enabling him to become more compassionate. His goal became to do all that he could to comfort those who experienced the loss of a loved one.

One of the most significant lessons he learned was how different cultures dealt with death and the grieving process. The one thing that helped to align him spiritually was the symbol on the top of a pole in the funeral home. The symbol could be spun to whatever symbol to match the religious path of the family. There was a cross on one side, a Star of David on another, so forth and so on. Sid called this his "Aha!" moment. He realized that we are all connected, no matter what our path is.

He said, "It is one spin. We're one people. No matter what culture you are, we're all on the same journey. We are all from the same family."

When Sid's mother died, he fell into depression and denial. The most painful event of his life is actually what opened the doors for his life to take a dramatic turn. He spent some time hiding from the feelings of loss that he felt. He tried to be strong for the rest of his family. After about a month, he finally let down his guard and had his moment of reckoning. He faced his grief head on.

Sid explained:

I enrolled in an intuitive development class. In one of the exercises, we had to go to an old house. We had to describe what we felt at the house. Others picked up on a fire and a murder, but I said all I could see was some cop who fell through the porch and broke his leg. I was actually disappointed because that was all I saw. Much to my surprise, the instructor called me days later. She worked for the police department. She learned that after our visit to the home, one of their deputies had gone to check on it. He fell through the porch and broke his leg. It was then that she informed me that my gift was to see ahead not behind. She offered to work with me more but eventually moved away. I continued studies on my own.

Eventually Sid began reading clients. He later studied under a parapsychology professor, Tom Clark, at University of New Orleans. Professor Clark offered healing circles in his home. The circle evolved into mediumship development. It was this mentor who told Sid that he saw him travelling to Sedona. He also saw Sid travelling to Camp Chesterfield in Indiana, a training facility for mediums. Three months later, he was invited by a friend to a Saints game in Phoenix, so he got his experience in Sedona. Soon, he ventured to Camp Chesterfield, where he had his first real contact with his mother.

He studied with a medium that had him write down two questions about two people who had passed on. He wrote down his questions, then folded them and held them in his hand. She sat across from him at a table and held his hand. She read the questions word for word without looking at them. She answered them. This is a form of mediumship that is called *billets*. She described Sid's mother to him as she came through. Sid could smell her scent. He also witnessed something called *spirit writing* while there. They put several blank cards and pens into a

Chapter One: The Medium

basket. They prayed over it. He could see that the cards were freshly opened index cards with nothing on them. After they prayed the contents were examined. Someone handed Sid a card. The card had a yellow rose on it. This was his mother's favorite flower.

Sid returned to New Orleans where he returned to college to pursue his career in nursing. He also resumed his studies under Tom Clark. Not long thereafter, Tom died. The night he died, Sid was returning home to New Orleans from Mississippi unaware at the time that Tom had passed. As he drove along the highway, he saw a gold light that shone right through his car. Sid saw Tom inside the gold light. Sid called Tom's partner. He was then informed that he had passed that night.

Sid went on to describe what angels and spirits look like to him.

He said:

Do you ever pump gas? Have you seen that waviness from the heat and the fumes rising from the nozzle? That's what it looks like. That's how I know they are in a room when I see that. They are a transparent form then they take on a figure. When I saw an actual spirit for the first time, I was in Chesterfield. I saw it and at the same time, this medium artist drew the exact spirit that I saw.

I saw something similar to that at the hospital, under the door of a room, so I ran into the nurse's station and hit the code button. Later, the other nurses asked me how I knew to call for help. I told them that I could see the angel coming for him. After that, every time someone was passing at the hospital, they would call me. I was there to hold their hand and make sure nobody passed alone. I had some heartbreaking experiences.

I had a young man come into the hospital this one time. I could see he was passing. He had come in to have a lump removed. He found out he had leukemia. He was only twenty-six years old. He died within forty-eight hours. He had to have tests run. The doctors would not give him pain medication because it would interfere with the tests. I held that man in my arms.

He looked at me and said, 'I'm going to die tonight.'

I told him that I would do everything I could to help him through this transition.

He passed at 2:00 AM.

There was another nurse who worked with me treating a patient who had coded. She hit code then she did this strange thing. She and I did this tunnel vision thing. I told her that she had to leave that room. Then I put some nitro paste on her that indicated that she had a heart issue. Most people, if they are not having a heart attack, will get a headache. She didn't. After much arguing with the doctor, I got him to agree to keep her in the hospital. Further testing proved that she had a cardiac issue that would have killed her on the way home had she left the hospital. She had this condition that you only get if you have birthed twins. The pressure puts a small rip in the heart. Over time it increases in size. She had the twins nine years before. It had been building up for all that time. She was so grateful to me she said, 'What can I do for you? I want to do something for you.'

I told her she could 'dance at my wedding' and she did. She and her husband flew in and danced at my wedding.

After his mother's death, Sid realized that he had ignored many signs pointing him to work as a medium. It was only after many years of soul searching was he truly able to embrace his gift. He had spent many years reading cards as a psychic but pushed aside mediumship readings until 2006, when he visited a friend who invited others over for readings. When Sid realized that there were about ten people who wanted readings, he excused himself to retrieve his cards. His friend stopped him and said, "Forget the cards. Just sit here and read the people."

He began reading them one by one; tuning into their energy. As he did this, he realized how clearly the spirits of their loved ones spoke to him. He began to see what their loved ones were wearing, how they died, and other details that he was able to relay to his sitters (persons receiving the message). This

Chapter One: The Medium

experience proved to him that there was some connection with Spirit that he had to explore.

It is no surprise that many mediums, like Sid, wind up on this path after a painful loss of a loved one or a near death experience of their own. Even though many have lifelong experiences with Spirit, it is often times the death of a close loved one that becomes the catalyst for pushing that person further along on the path of a medium.

Sid's journey has been one of exploration. He believes that we are here to experience and enjoy the journey. He also believes that there is more than one journey sometimes.

When asked about reincarnation, he replied:

Yes, I believe in reincarnation but our goal is to come back as better people. Our ultimate goal is to become that higher spiritual consciousness so we can become one with our maker. Does that mean when we come back is it always better? No. Just because you come in on one level of energy doesn't mean it is going to go up. It could go down or it could remain the same.

He also expressed that love and selflessness were the key to connecting with Spirit.

His philosophy is:

As long as you have love in your heart, the world is at your fingertips.

Chapter Two
Becoming the Tube

Once open to the spirit realm, you see the world through different eyes. In the movie, *Stir of Echoes*, Kevin Bacon's character became an open channel after a half-baked hypnosis session conducted by a friend, during a party. Once he was given the hypnotic suggestion that his mind was *open to everything*, he began to see spirits. Everyone has a sixth sense. Each one of us has the ability to communicate with other realms although probably not to the extent of what is portrayed in movies. I have always found it easy to see, hear, and feel spirits. But until I met Sid, I did not realize that what I was experiencing was only a small portion of the spirit world. I easily tuned into earthbound entities. I had conducted spirit communication for two decades on paranormal investigations. The spirits with whom I communicated on these investigations had left their physical bodies, and had remained in the tunnel, not having crossed over into the light, for whatever reason. Although I had many experiences with connection on a deeper level, it was not constant. It was also very random. I had little control over it. This is typical for most people until they fine tune the ability. Sometimes, it was easy to connect but other times, it seemed to elude me somewhat. The best way to describe it was as if I had phone calls to the other side but sometimes did not have a good connection.

I had spent many years in religions that revolved around communication with spirits. In certain spiritual paths, we hold spiritual *misas* (masses for the dead) which are specifically designed to develop mediumship. During the misa, prayers are said to open the door to the spirit world. We sit listening, sometimes for hours, for messages. This practice is done specifically to attune one for mediumship. But once outside these parameters, my mind would get cluttered with worldly thoughts. I often became too caught up in the left brain. More often than not, I tuned into spirits that had not fully crossed over since they were still vibrating very close to our physical vibration.

What many people do not realize is that a psychic and a medium are not always one and the same person. A psychic is an individual who connects with psychic energy around a person, place, or object. A psychic obtains information from that energy. A medium has the ability to communicate with those who are fully in the spirit world. Mediums not only validate that life continues after the physical death, but also prove that those who have crossed over continue to learn. They also have the same personality traits they did in their physical existence.

All mediums are psychic, but not all psychics are mediums. Contrary to popular belief, the medium has no control over who chooses to communicate. We retain our personalities on the other side as well as our free will, so it is Spirit who chooses when and with whom to communicate. A medium can try to contact a specific person during a session but it is ultimately up to Spirit who comes through.

While researching Near Death Experiences (NDEs), I learned that most experiencers described passing through a tunnel of some type with a bright light at the end. Most of these people mentioned that there were some souls in the tunnel who were not moving forward. These souls choose to remain on the physical plane, or at least in some space between the spirit world and the physical. The tunnel is the portal or doorway between our physical world and the afterlife. There are many levels on the other side. The higher the vibration of the spirit, the closer to God's consciousness it is. The lower the vibration, the closer to our physical world it is. The higher vibrational spirits are free to travel through the various levels of existence. They may choose to communicate with loved ones to comfort them, give specific messages, or just to say hello. Often, if the sitter is not open to

Chapter Two: Becoming the Tube

receiving direct messages, the spirit will use a third party, a medium, to convey messages.

The medium receives signs, symbols, and other information through the senses that are given to confirm that the message is indeed coming from a departed loved one rather than from the auric field of the individual. These are called *memory links*. Many times when a spirit communicates, the first thing a medium will detect is the sex and relationship of that spirit to the sitter. The next reference point addressed is how the person died which is usually the first thing that will be recognizable by the sitter. The memory link is a memory shared between the sitter and the spirit that validates that the message could only come from that loved one. The memory can be something recent, or a shared experience from many years prior to death. Sometimes the memory link is something that the sitter was either too young to remember or had possibly forgotten. Validation will come later through a third party or a photograph.

I read for one sitter whose grandfather came through during a psychic reading at a fair. There was no intent on anyone's part to bring in her loved one. But, like so often it happens, if Spirit wants to convey a message, a message will come through to the medium. When he stepped forward, I immediately sensed that it was her grandfather.

Although she did not remember him, he remembered her. He appeared to me as a faded black and white photograph, wearing high fishing boots, standing on a wharf, holding a large fish he had just caught. He also showed me a game that was at an amusement park that had closed down long before the sitter was born. It was called *The Fishing Game*. It was a circular metal pool with rushing water where small children could catch a wooden fish on the pole and get a prize. Of course, the sitter was not familiar with the scene so I told her to ask her mother if it made sense to her. She returned later to tell me, in person, that her mother validated *The Fishing Game* confirming that her father had taken her there often as a child.

The sitter emailed me later that evening. She attached a photo that her mother had shown her. It was her grandfather, in a faded black and white photo, with the fish, exactly as I had seen him during the session. He showed me himself as that specific photo because he knew that she would later be able to validate it through her mother. There was no mistake that he had indeed communicated. Several days later, she emailed again to tell me that her son went to a birthday party. The party favors were small plastic fishing poles with several plastic fish, called of course, *The Fishing Game*. Again, this was no coincidence.

Once I had fully familiarized myself with how to properly blend with Spirit by raising my vibration, I connected on a higher level thus able to obtain information direct from Spirit that could be validated. The more I worked on this, the more consistent it became. My communication was clearer than ever before. This would explain why in the past, I could not always reach my daughter. I had not been properly raising my vibration rate enough to reach a spirit at her level of existence. Additionally, my grief held me back considerably. My emotions had been too erratic to properly connect on that higher level. Any kind of negative emotion such as grief, anger, jealousy, hate, will make it difficult to raise our vibration enough to properly connect with Spirit.

A true medium connects to spirits who are beyond the tunnel by raising their personal vibration rate to resonate with that of the spirit realm. The vibration rate of Spirit is faster than our vibration on the physical plane. In order to reach that level of vibration, one must do this by various methods such as music, singing, chanting, writing, or drawing. This is the reason in spiritual rituals, church services, séances, etc. participants sing and music is played. In many early tribal traditions, drumming and chanting were often used to raise the vibration rate. Once the vibration was raised, the medium then became what Sid Patrick calls *the tube*. The medium is merely a vehicle through which those on the other side can send messages to those on the physical plane. The medium can do this while working face to face with a client one on one, during gallery readings for numerous people, during a séance, or even long distance when the client isn't even in front of them.

Chapter Two: Becoming the Tube

During the months following my daughter's death, I visited more than one medium, as I needed constant validation. Although Sid Patrick made initial contact with her, it was not enough for me. I wanted more validation and communication. I saw her every day of her life. I wanted to continue to communicate with her like I did when she was here.

For most mediums, there is a certain routine that is followed. Before any session begins, the medium usually explains how communication works for him/her. Generally, the medium has spent a great deal of time working with Spirit to attune to that vibration rate. Many mediums have a doorkeeper who is often a deceased family member or a spirit guide who assists from the other side to open the door of communication between the living and the dead. Once the doorkeeper has been asked to allow communication, the medium can then give messages from the other side. One medium, Freddie Rivera, reached numerous family members on the other side, including my father who had died almost forty years earlier.

My father had been a very stern man who shared an emotionally distanced relationship with me. During a phone reading session with Freddie, my father expressed sorrow for the distance that he had put between us during his life. He also expressed that he was proud of me. He encouraged me to write more. Sometimes, mediums will hear only partial names or syllables. Freddie told me that my father was with two other people. He said the woman had an "M" name like Margaret. He also said the number four. He then asked me if I knew someone named Robert.

As it turned out, my father had four siblings, one of whom was his sister Margaret. My Aunt Margaret was married to my Uncle Bob (Robert). He then said there was someone with a name that began with "L." At the time, this made no sense to me other than that my maiden name began with "L." Later that evening, I remembered that my father's other sister was my Aunt Lily. Freddie also heard a name like Anna. This meant nothing to me in that moment but I later learned from a cousin that my Aunt Lily's full name was Anna Lillian. It is very common to obtain validation after the reading has taken place. Sometimes we become so overwhelmed with emotions when receiving messages from the other side that we are not completely on point with validating facts. Many people simply forget details, only to remember later or to be reminded when recounting the reading to other family members. In my case, my parents were a bit older when I was born. They both died when I was young. My aunts and uncles were also in their mid-lives when I was born so many of the messages I received were from people that I had not heard from in over thirty years. It is easy to forget minor details in such circumstances.

My mother then stepped forward. Freddie described her in the finest of details. I was pleased to learn that my parents were still a couple and soul mates on the other side. They had been together since they were very young. They had spent their entire lives together. I had read in many sources that some married couples continue as couples together in the afterlife. This seemed to validate that school of thought. Freddie told me that my mother spoke of someone named Kathy, and he was confused as to whether it was a "C" or a "K" name. My mother's name was Carrie. My birth name was Kathy.

Mediums often mention months when delivering a message. A month might represent the birthday of someone or the month that someone passed. During my reading with Freddie, my parents said something about March. I believed it represented my daughter, Stephanie, whose birthday was March 1st. Freddie, like the other mediums that I had consulted, immediately tuned into Stephanie's child-like nature. He asked me if she was special. Although she was almost thirty when she died, her energy was like a young teen. Also, spirits will sometimes show the medium things that the loved one will recognize as being them. One medium saw sidewalk chalk, baby dolls, and stuffed animals, showing her that she was communicating with either a child or someone who was child-like.

Freddie really amazed me when he delivered what he felt was a strange message from Stephanie. He hesitated then said, "I

Chapter Two: Becoming the Tube

don't know why she is talking about pizza, but she's telling me to say it. She said, *I like pizza, too, you know. Bring me a piece.*"

Unbeknownst to Freddie, I was in my car, on my mobile phone, sitting outside of a pizza restaurant, waiting for my granddaughter to pick up an order. There was absolutely no way that he could have possibly known that. Stephanie knew where I was. He also said it exactly the way she would have. This was not a coincidence; he had communicated with her. It was as if I was on a direct call to her.

My reading with Freddie was on November 2, 2013. I had spent that day with several others, cleaning graves at a local cemetery. November 2nd is All Souls Day in the Catholic Church, as well as in other traditions. We honor the souls who have passed on to continue their spiritual lessons in hopes of ascending to their highest potential. We clean graves of those who are in need of attention. Holt Cemetery in New Orleans is a city cemetery for those who cannot afford private plots. Some of the graves are very old, and in dire need of upkeep. I had chosen to clean the grave of an unnamed baby boy, who had died a few years before.

After cleaning the graves, the group returned to the spiritual temple to honor the dead on an altar. We lit candles, made offerings of food and libation. We said prayers for the souls of those in the cemetery. In addition to honoring this unknown child and others who were buried there, I remembered my own unnamed child who was lost to miscarriage in 1982. That baby would have been my middle child. In the 1980s, babies who died that early were unceremoniously disposed of by the hospital. Bereaved mothers were given little sympathy for their loss. It was assumed that the mother was "young and able to have another child." Although I grieved deeply for this child, it was hardly enough. I did the socially accepted thing at the time. I pushed my grief inside. I remained heartbroken over the loss until Stephanie's birth, when I was finally able to move beyond the pain. I always wondered what that child would have been like.

A mother never gets over the death of a child regardless of the child's age or even if the death occurred prior to the birth. Although it was too early to determine the sex of the baby, I had always imagined that it was a boy. I had picked out the name Christopher, but not a girl's name, even though it might have been a girl for all I knew. I shared the story with my godparents. We called the baby in the unmarked grave Christopher Doe.

I mentioned to the others who were present that I often wondered if Stephanie met her unborn sibling on the other side. Later that evening, when I spoke to Freddie, that question was answered. Stephanie gave a message that she did not have a brother in heaven but a sister. Later that night Stephanie appeared to me in a dream. She informed me that her sister's name was Jennifer. When my oldest daughter was a young child, she always wanted a baby sister named Jennifer. When I had Stephanie, she even called her Jennifer when she was first born. It took a while for her to grow accustomed to calling her Stephanie. All throughout Stephanie's life, she always said she had two sisters. I would always correct her.

I would tell her, "You have only one sister."

She would always argue, "No, I have two."

This would explain why the butterflies sometimes appear in pairs. There was one from Stephanie and another from Jennifer. In fact, it validated something another medium had told me in a reading several months before the one I received from Freddie. As she gave messages from Stephanie, she kept saying something about someone with a "J" name. At the time, this meant nothing to me but after this recent reading, I realized that Stephanie was trying to tell me about Jennifer. I learned from later readings that Jennifer had decided that she did not want to come to this world. She felt bad that I was sad over her decision.

The one message that Stephanie did give through several mediums that was very important was that she was where she came from. She said, "This is where we come from. I am home."

Evidential validation of Spirit is something that occurs when the sitter finally makes sense of something that was not readily

Chapter Two: Becoming the Tube

recognized during the reading. Sid Patrick says that the job of the medium is to validate the existence of life after death. Validation is important to further solidify this to the bereaved. The medium's role is to prove that the lost loved one still exists. This is very important for healing grief. Sometimes validation comes in bits and pieces. Sid Patrick had mentioned a green feather to me in his reading. I had completely forgotten that several years before, someone gave me a green feather pen. I had placed it on the top of a bookcase then forgot about it. Many months after my reading, I awakened to find it in my foyer, lying on the floor. Then later, it appeared mysteriously again outside my bedroom door on Christmas Eve. I have no explanation for how it got in my path on those two occasions other than it *apported*. *Apportation* occurs when an object or matter dematerializes in one place simultaneously materializing in another. It is a form of physical phenomenon occurring during physical séances. He also mentioned in his reading to me, that my friend who traveled with Stephanie, Gary, said that I would see a doorway with three circles on it. It was many months later, when I realized that there were three circles above each doorway of the St. Louis Cathedral in the French Quarter. I had stood in front of it many nights, for almost two decades, never noticing them. Then suddenly, they caught my eye, giving me more validation from Spirit.

It is important that the medium is empathetic with his sitters. Working with the grief-stricken is extremely sensitive. It is important that the medium works with complete respect and humility when connecting to spirits of loved ones. It should always be done in the best interest of the sitter. Sid Patrick teaches that the medium must always remain selfless and void of ego.

"It's not about you," he reminds medium trainees, "Our egos want to be right. It doesn't matter if you are right or wrong. A medium is a servant of Spirit. Spirit will not show you what is not supposed to be seen. It is nothing personal."

He explained that it does not matter whether you are right or wrong. He knows that what he is shown comes from Spirit but also knows that it is not his job to analyze it or know what it means. His job is to deliver the message to the sitter. Often times, the sitter will validate later, even in cases when initially they do not understand the message being relayed.

After working with several mediums in addition to Sid, I committed myself to further developing my relationship with Spirit through my mediumship. When Sid originally made contact with my daughter shortly after her death, he said that she emphasized that I needed to *move on*. I realized that she did not want me to move on as in forgetting her life. She wanted me to grow spiritually so I could feel more comfortable with her transitioning to the other side, long before I was ready for her to go. I became ever more determined to remain in close contact with her.

I had grown accustomed to her signs and symbols that she had been sending to me. It had become like a game. It was as if she enjoyed seeing if I would recognize the signs. One of her more humorous signs was a huge green grasshopper that she sent to me while I worked in the French Quarter. Grasshoppers are uncommon there. I had never seen them in that area in my life. But one evening in Pirate's Alley, a huge grasshopper flew at me several times. I became so frightened that I had to run back to my car to get away from it.

The following night, as I exited my car to go back to work, I looked up onto the rafters of the gallery above me only to see the huge insect again. Terrified of large flying bugs, I ran into a nearby courtyard to escape the frightening creature. After a while, I needed to make a trip to the ladies room. When I turned into the alcove to the restroom area, there was the grasshopper on the door.

Later that evening, as I walked back to the alley, I saw a huge green flying insect in flight just feet ahead of me. It landed on the gas lamp above my head.

On the following evening, a large grasshopper appeared at the shop where all three of my granddaughters worked. It flew inside the building, then appeared on the car after they closed shop. We

Chapter Two: Becoming the Tube

all agreed that it had to be one of Stephanie's "gifts" that she sent to us.

Chapter Three
The Circle

Having worked with the paranormal and energy healing for more than twenty years, I was no stranger to psychic energy. I understood how it worked. The life force of universal energy that connects all things had been first introduced to me as *chi,* through my studies of Chinese medicine and martial arts, then later as *prana* in my yoga studies. Psychic energy is also called mental energy. Our thoughts, feelings, and beliefs are very powerful. As this mental energy flows from our minds into the astral plane, it eventually returns to us as physical phenomena. It is the basis of all magical practices, as well as philosophies such as positive thinking, manifesting, and the law of attraction. Wherever we focus this mental energy, we manifest our own realities to a large degree. All energy is vibration. The slower the vibration, the more physical or solid something becomes. Quantum physics teaches us that even those things that appear as solid are merely very slowly moving particles, giving only the illusion of physicality. The transfer of mental energy from one mind to another is called *telepathy*. Spirits of those who have left their physical body can still communicate telepathically with the living. This is mental mediumship.

The mental séances that Sid Patrick held were different from anything that I had experienced in the past. He was a follower of the Spiritualist Church that arose from the 19th century Spiritualist Movement. The church promotes mediumship and enforces the belief of life continuing after death.

I had been involved in séances with a follower of Theosophy, then through Spiritism, both of which were a bit different. Theosophy was established by Helena Blavatsky in the early

1800s as a religion, combining both Eastern and Western esoteric teachings, including doctrine on life after death. Spiritism differs from Spiritualism in that it is not a religion, but more of a philosophy. Like Spiritualism, Spiritism believes in the immortal spirit and other dimensions of existence. Spiritism principals are often found in Caribbean religions.

Like other traditions, the Spiritualist séance incorporates music and singing to raise the vibration of the room. But before any of that can occur, many sessions of mental medium circles must be attended. During these circles, prospective mediums gather to attune themselves to becoming sensitive to spiritual communication. Regardless of how adept a medium is, gathering in circle to commune with Spirit is necessary to maintain the relationship with Spirit. Circles are generally done on a regular schedule, same place, day of week, and time. It is an appointment not only between mediums but with Spirit. It does require commitment.

Before one can begin to participate in actual mediumship, he/she must have an understanding of the various ways that Spirit can manifest and communicate. We use our senses to experience this. The use of our senses as a way of experiencing spiritual phenomena is called *The Clairs*.

Clairvoyance literally means *clear vision*. It is the ability to gain information psychically by seeing something. The clairvoyant will see spirits appear in lights, in the third eye, or even in dreams. Some psychics are clairvoyant in that they can see events before they take place. *Clairsentience* is knowledge by feeling. This is felt as a sensation in the body. Those people who get a *gut feeling* about something are experiencing clairsentience. *Clairaudience* is acquiring information by means of hearing. The clairaudient medium will hear voices, or music, or sounds as a means of communication. *Clairessence* is using the sense of smell to obtain information. Similarly *clairgustance* is perceived through tastes. Sometimes our loved ones will make their presence known by presenting a familiar scent or flavor. Very often people will smell the aroma of someone's favorite perfume or flower, and know that they are nearby.

Chapter Three: The Circle

Claircognizance is the ability to know something without a physical explanation as to why. Often, mediums receive information in this way from spirits. Most mediums utilize all of the *Clairs* when working with the other side.

Remote viewing is a technique in which the viewer relies solely on the subconscious mind to give information. Remote viewing techniques can be valuable to a medium as it facilitates all of the *Clairs,* all at once very quickly before the conscious mind has a chance to question any of the information being processed. The technique trains the medium to use his/her senses without analyzing it with the conscious mind.

As with many disciplines, the remote viewer learns to turn off the inner dialogue and the conscious mind relying solely on the senses and the subconscious. The objective is to be completely disengaged from all thoughts in order to be in tune with the subconscious. In numerous disciplines such as Tai Chi, yoga, and meditation, the object is to ignore the conscious mind and just "be." This is more easily said than done. The conscious mind does not like being turned off nor does it like being wrong. The remote viewer uses their senses to tap into information directly from the subconscious mind or the higher self. Through continual exercising of this technique, the individual can become more sensitive to psychic phenomena and/or messages from Spirit.

Sid explained how mediumship works:

Mediumship ability depends on how open your right brain is to the level of creativity where you are able to sense these things. A nurse with empathy can look into a room and tell you exactly what is going on with that patient without even looking at the patient. It is understanding the Clairs and using your senses in order to be sensitive to the energies around you. The medium must be able to take in that energy and process it.

When someone was dying in a hospital, Sid would open the window because people used to believe that the spirit would leave through the window.

Kalila Smith & Sid Patrick

There was one famous football player who was passing from a disease process. I was called into his room. I looked for the energy in the room. I could tell by the energy present that he probably had about an hour left. So I woke him up and got the family into the room. Within about an hour and a half, he did pass.

There had been many times that Sid had walked into a room and saw death on a patient. A former boyfriend had an unusual blackness in his eyes. He passed within two years of Sid seeing this. Sid has also seen the energy leaving the bodies of patients during surgery or shortly after.

****

During my first mental mediumship circle with Sid, I felt the energy of a woman standing between myself and him, as we sat in a circle with others. She appeared as an icy presence, moving in between our chairs. Immediately I sensed that she was a mother or grandmother figure. I began to see pictures in my mind's eye of a woman dressed in 1960s era house dress with an apron. My own mother dressed like that when I was a child. When spirits communicate they use what is called *symbology*. They present symbols that are familiar to the medium that represent certain things. Without a doubt the woman present was not my mother, but I kept seeing my mother's clothing and her old kitchen when I was a child. These symbols represented a mother to me. But yet I picked up that she was more of a mother figure, like a grandmother or caretaker. I saw scenes of this woman baking biscuits for a small boy. I also smelled flowers. I kept getting a vision of a large bush with beautiful clusters of blue flowers. This memory link was familiar to Sid, realizing immediately that the woman present was the woman who had been a nanny to him as a child. Once the memory link is established, the medium then delivers a message to the sitter from their loved one. Sometimes the message is merely to let the

Chapter Three: The Circle

person know that the loved one continues to survive after death and is watching over those still here.

There are times when Spirit is very literal. A medium will see or hear something very precise such as when Freddie heard Stephanie talk about the pizza. One medium literally saw a paper plate with a hot dog on it. The week before, I had put that exact thing on Stephanie's altar. So, although symbols are the most common, the message can be literal.

Some symbols will be replaced with others, depending on what is available. Not all symbols simply pop into your head. Some are seen in the physical world. Stephanie often used butterflies to communicate her presence with me. When butterfly season was over, she switched to a moth. I was sitting in my car outside of a smoothie bar, discussing a Christmas party with my granddaughters, when from behind the building came a huge moth. The moth was brightly coloured and flying in a zigzag formation. Moths are nowhere near as graceful as butterflies but clearly she was making this one move as much as it could to resemble a butterfly. It flew in a figure eight pattern over a sign that said "Happy Holidays," then flew back around the building. She used what was available to convey her message.

Another important practice for the medium is *sitting with Spirit*. This is similar to meditation except while meditating, the focus is on the self. Sitting with Spirit, sometimes called *blending*, is an open invitation with Spirit. It is essential to make an appointment with Spirit to communicate. During this interaction, we teach Spirit how we can understand their symbols. It is important to be consistent. It is best to schedule the same time, same place to meet with Spirit and get them accustomed to meeting at that time. The more Spirit gets to know how we recognize their signs and symbols, the easier it becomes to receive messages and translate those messages to someone else.

Sometimes a sitter will seek the help of a medium to attempt to communicate with a particular loved one, only to be surprised by a visit from someone that they did not expect to hear from. After Sid read me the first time, I shared my experience with someone who had recently lost a loved one in an accident. Still in shock from the loss, she visited Sid in hope of communicating with her lost love. But instead of him coming through, she received a surprise visit from her mother. The problem was that my friend had two mothers, a birth mother and an adoptive mother. She was not sure which one had come through.

Sid began to describe a mother figure coming through. He described a short, small framed woman with short hair. Both of her "mothers" fit that description. Every time Sid would attempt a memory link, my friend responded that it could be either of the women coming forth. Finally, he heard, "Tell her pretzels and beer."

He was very hesitant but eventually said, "This sounds really strange but she said to tell you *pretzels and beer*."

Suddenly my friend realized that it was her adoptive mother who was coming through to her. This mother had suffered with a long term disease. For many months could not eat certain foods. Then in her final days, she wanted to have a party with her family and enjoy, one last time, some of her favorite things. She feasted on pretzels, meats, cheeses, and beer. Even though it was not the person she set out to communicate with, it was apparently the message the sitter needed at the time.

Sometimes, deceased family members, who were not our favorites, will come through to apologize or settle unfinished business. The medium is only the messenger. The messages that come through may not always be the ones we want, but they are always the ones we need. Spirit does not make mistakes nor will Spirit waste a moment of time. The medium must learn to trust what is being seen, heard, or felt from Spirit.

When asked what he believed the spirit world was like, Sid explained:

In Spiritualism, we validate that there is life after death. It's all based on scientific fact. Thoughts and actions are all energy. Energy never dies. It all transforms from potential energy to kinetic. We all go to the same place. Heaven is not so much a place as it is level of consciousness. Rather than a place which is below or above us, it is a dimension. The various planes of

Chapter Three: The Circle

existence are much like an onion and each peel is a layer of another dimension.

I believe that we go before our maker, then, to school to learn what we did wrong. We learn how we can better improve ourselves and grow spiritually. Spirits that come through mediumship are there to help you. When you cross over, you become part of that infinite all-knowing consciousness. I believe that you go before God's court, then, to a place of study and learning. I truly believe that we learn about our life and our life's purpose. We hang around our loved ones to help them on their journeys to get a better understanding of who they are. Then, it comes our turn to come back. During our life in the physical world, we can raise our consciousness or lower it.

My idea of hell would be not realizing that we can change our level of consciousness to a higher one. But death is not an ending, it is a beginning.

****

On Halloween, it is believed, in various cultures and religions, that the veil between the world of the living and the dead is the thinnest. On Halloween night 2013, a group of about twenty people gathered at the Metaphysical Resource Center after accompanying me on a ghost tour of the French Quarter. At the center, we formed a large seated circle. Unlike what is portrayed in movies or in other spiritual paths, there was no hand holding. Everyone was asked to sit with their legs uncrossed, feet on the floor and hands on their laps facing upwards. The lights were turned off. We all sat quietly as Sid said the opening prayer, asking for God's protection against any spirit not walking in His light. When the prayers were over, Sid quietly instructed someone in the room to turn on the player. Suddenly, the dark was overcome with the sounds of music. Everyone sang along as best they could to raise the vibration rate of the room, in the hopes of drawing in the spirits of those who wished to communicate. I felt something touching my legs from time to time. The only thing that I compare it to was what it felt like when a small fish would swim close by in the ocean. I also felt the sensation of spider webs brushing across my face. The room became markedly colder.

Before long, white, misty ectoplasm filled the room as the temperature dropped even more significantly. Most of us witnessed tiny sparkles of lights whirling around within the glowing mist. The thicker the fog became, the more activity could be noted. Sid described seeing a man with horses. The woman sitting next to me validated this by recognizing the spirit as her father. She cried as she called out to him. Suddenly, Sid was distracted by another visitor.

He blurted out, "I'm seeing horses then suddenly a unicorn is running through the scene. Kalila, I think Stephanie is here."

Stephanie loved to paint. One of the last pictures she painted was of a unicorn. If he was seeing a unicorn, it had to be her.

One participant who was sitting at the far right side of the room, called out to me, "Kalila, what is going on in front of you? I see something swirling in front of you."

I felt my daughter's energy. I smelled the familiar fragrance of her floral body spray that she loved to wear. An icy presence swirled and swayed in front of me as Beyonce's *All the Single Ladies* played. Tiny flickers of lights danced around in front of me as I held my hands out feeling her cold presence. She was all around me.

After the séance, Sid explained the mental medium séance:

I think that the world is evolving at such a fast rate these days with all the technology that we have in society. Because Spirit is energy based it is able to communicate a lot better today than it could when the Fox sisters, some of the first spiritualist ever, began publicizing their findings. The veil is becoming thinner. I do believe that people are becoming born with a higher consciousness. We are all connected; every person, every plant, every bird, the sea, the sky. It's all one big picture. For me, it's learning how to communicate with Spirit.

Chapter Three: The Circle

The mental séance was only a prelude to what would occur when we attempted to obtain physical phenomena. The best was yet to come.

Chapter Four
Getting Physical

Mental mediumship is only one way that mediums communicate with the other side. Physical mediumship takes the experience to a completely different level. Mental medium sessions are used for one-on-one private consultation, gallery style readings, or the mental séance as described in the previous chapter. A gallery reading or *platform* is a group of people who receive random messages from a medium. The less people present the higher the likelihood of receiving a message from a loved one. Spirits do not perform on demand. The medium has no control over who steps forth with messages, if any at all. In large galleries, there are more spirits coming through than time for the medium to relay the messages. The ones who do receive messages are generally those who need it the most. The smaller the group, the more personal the setting is. It is also more likely that everyone in the room will receive a message. The medium's doorkeeper keeps order on the other side but does not determine who steps forth.

Mediumship is based on the universal laws of energy. Energy is the universal force which encompasses all things. In order for the medium to connect with Spirit for communication, the vibration rate must be raised. The higher the vibration of the entity, the brighter the auric or energetic field of that entity and the more fluid it can express itself to the medium.

The skeptic would argue that psychic energy cannot exist because it is unseen. However, many forms of energy are not seen, yet we know that they exist: microwaves, radio waves, sound, x-rays, etc. Thoughts and emotions are unseen, but they are forms of energy, from the mind, as waves. Thought forms vibrate from the astral plane to the physical plane. This is why much of what happens in our lives is of our own creation. Thoughts, desires, beliefs that are transmitted into the energetic plane eventually manifest on the physical plane. All energy eventually returns to where it was first created. The energy that you put out eventually returns to you. During mediumship, there is a three-way connection of energy between Spirit, medium, and sitter.

Physical mediumship has many forms such as trance mediumship, physical phenomena such as apportation of objects and movement of physical objects caused by Spirit, table tipping, communication boards, psychometry, trance mediumship, and automatic writing, to name a few. I have worked quite a bit with psychometry for many years. Psychometry is the act of feeling or sensing energy of an inanimate object. I had also experienced a form of channeling when I wrote *Afterlife Mysteries Revealed*. Much of that book was written while in altered states of consciousness, as Stephanie channeled through me. Often times, while writing that book, my hands were typing faster than my brain could keep up as though on automatic pilot.

I also channeled Stephanie to some degree when I decided to paint for the first time. I visited an art studio where artists used a template that was already on the canvas. I painted a peacock for my oldest daughter as a gift. The project took me three hours to complete. All the while, I analyzed it and changed my mind about which colours I liked on it. Then when it was done, something prompted me to also paint a butterfly.

My hand took off as though it was not attached to my body. I completed the butterfly in thirty minutes. Stephanie was extremely artistic and I knew that it was really her and not I who had painted it.

Chapter Four: Getting Physical

Regardless of which path one goes down in physical mediumship, developing the mental mediumship is the key to a good physical medium. Mediumship development is a process that takes time and patience. The medium must develop a relationship with Spirit. It is a journey for all parties involved. Just as relationships for us here take years to cultivate and develop, it is the same for our relationship with Spirit.

Sid gave me his criteria for physical phenomena:

Physical mediumship requires validation. Someone other than the medium must validate that the spirit coming through is their departed loved one. This can be distinguished by the way they talk, the rate of the speech, and the character and personality of the person must come through. With physical phenomena, all sitters must be aware of it. Physical phenomena can be apports (physical objects appearing from nowhere), it can be a direct voice channeled through a medium, but it must have validation in order for it to be evidential. It has to be something that can be proven. It can be something that no one present knows at the time, but if you research it you can find out about it.

Spirituality is natural. The religious preference of the sitter is not important. The love and relationship of the spirit to the sitter is what matters.

In physical circle groups, cohesiveness and commitment to Spirit are essential. Even if only one person in the group develops, all are blessed by the experience. The séance room is a laboratory for both the mediums and Spirit, and must always be treated as such. To be a sitter and receive messages from Spirit is an honor and needed for physical phenomena to occur.

Spirit has the capability to do anything, as long as we allow and accept. True evidential mediumship occurs when the sitter does not understand the message at the time, but later finds the meaning. Trance is a form a physical mediumship and you can give evidential proof of a concise message. There should be some evidence. Speaking in trance is not proof, but what is spoken is.

Communication with spirits via physical mediumship is nothing new. Swedish scientist/inventor Emanuel Swedenborg (1688-1772) was the first European to popularize the idea that communication was possible with spiritual beings other than those of a higher order, such as angels or saints. His dreams and visions of the afterlife began at age fifty-three on Easter weekend, April 6, 1744. He received an epiphany from God, giving him visions of both Heaven and Hell. In his first spiritual work, *The Heavenly Doctrine*, he spoke to angels, demons, and spirits of those who were once human. He was the first to note that there were various planes to the spirit realm. He wrote eighteen books on the afterlife in the following years. Several months before his death on March 29, 1772, he wrote a letter to Methodist church founder, John Wesley. In this letter, he told Wesley the date that he would enter the afterlife. After his death, Wesley went on to study all of Swedenborg's works.

Swedenborg's last statement on the afterlife was on his deathbed, where he announced, "As truly as you see me before your eyes, so true is everything that I have written and I could have said more had it been permitted. When you enter eternity you will see everything, then you and I shall have much to talk about."

American clairvoyant, Andrew Jackson Davis (1826-1910), is credited with being one of the fathers of Modern Spiritualism. He grew up impoverished in New York, the son of a shoemaker. He became interested in mesmerism (hypnotism). Through attending seminars on the subject, he discovered that in a trance state, he could diagnose medical disorders in others. Through his mind's eye, in an altered state, he could literally see through the physical body and directly at the organs inside.

Chapter Four: Getting Physical

In 1844, he experienced an out of body trance state. He found himself 40 miles away in the Catskills Mountains. It was there that he envisioned the apparitions of the philosopher Galen and Emanuel Swedenborg, both of whom were dead.

This transcendent experience had a tremendous impact on Davis. He began to travel giving lectures on the subject of Spiritualism. It was through these travels that he met renowned mesmerist, Dr. Lyons. In the trance state, Davis dictated to him, *The Principles of Nature: Her Divine Revelations and A Voice to Mankind.*

The process took fifteen months to complete. Due to his lack of education, it is presumed that Davis was truly channeling from a higher source, perhaps even Swedenborg himself. *Principles of Nature* was published in 1847. Despite his lack of early education, he wrote over thirty books on the subject. He eventually obtained a medical degree.

In 1848, Margaretta and Kate Fox were the first in America to popularize *spirit tapping* as a form of communication with the dead. They claimed to communicate with the spirit of man named Charles B. Rosna. He conveyed to the sisters that he had been murdered and buried in the basement of their home.

The family had moved to the house in December of the previous year and the house was reputed to be haunted by the previous owner. In March 1848, the family began to experience loud noises in the house such that the beds shook.

The sisters began to communicate with the spirit by asking it to repeat rapping sounds that they made. In time, they used these raps to ask particular questions of the spirit. In 1904, The Boston Journal confirmed that the skeletal remains of a man had been found buried beneath the basement of the house. I learned from a friend, renowned occult expert Dr. Raymond Buckland that along with the remains of Mr. Rosna, there was a tin box that had belonged to the man. It is on display in the Lilydale Museum in

New York. There is a photo of the box in Dr. Buckland's book, *Buckland's Book of Spirit Communication*.

Although Spiritualism faded in the United States, The Spiritualist Movement became extremely popular in Great Britain. Entire families not only engaged in organized séances but formed medium circles and held weekly meetings along with Sunday dinner. One of the pioneers in early British Spiritualism was Arthur Conan Doyle. In 1887, he joined the Society for Psychical Research, which consisted of scholars dedicated to using scientific means to validate paranormal and Spiritualists' claims. It brought spirituality together with science, which had always been debated. Doyle immersed himself in Spiritualism after the tragic death of his wife and later, his son, followed by his two brothers. For a time, he befriended American illusionist, Harry Houdini. Houdini had also become attracted to Spiritualism after the death of his mother. Oddly enough, it was this mutual interest that brought them together and the same that eventually caused the demise of the friendship. Houdini became disenchanted with Spiritualism after mediums failed to contact his late mother. Doyle, on the other hand, became involved with the movement. Their differences on the subject drove a wedge between them that was irreparable. Despite many who disbelieved and tried to prove fraud in the area of physical mediumship, it continued to thrive in Great Britain, even to this day.

There are many forms of physical mediumship. Table tipping, spirit manifestation, apportation of objects, and trance mediumship are various forms of physical manifestation of Spirit, through a medium. Channeling, healing, automatic writing, and mediumistic art are all various types of trance. Materialization trance is where the medium physically produces ectoplasm (physical Spirit matter that appears as a light fog or mist) internally and emits it through the nose, mouth, or other orifices for the purpose of manifesting apparitions of deceased loved ones

Chapter Four: Getting Physical

on the physical plane. Some have even formed full-bodied apparitions who have communicated to sitters. This form of mediumship is highly specialized. It is something that should not be taken lightly. There are two types of ectoplasm, that produced by the medium, and that produced by Spirit.

A visiting trance healer from England described such manifestations to Sid and me. She admitted to seeing ectoplasm coming out of a medium that formed the apparition of a small man who approached her and offered his wrist for her to feel his pulse. She touched what felt like living flesh with a pulse. The man spoke to her and assured her that he was real. She said other figures appeared giving messages. One was a woman who disappeared into the floor, leaving only her head out, still talking.

"In physical mediumship settings there are controls," Sid said, "Anytime trance is involved the medium must be in good health, because it does weaken the system. The ectoplasm is believed to be produced in the thyroid and pancreas. There are also sugar highs and lows involved with physical mediumship."

Some physical mediums are able to produce physical movement of inanimate objects. Sid was conducting a physical séance in Dallas when a small statue of Buddha manifested out of nowhere and crashed onto the living room floor of his friend's home, in another state. Sid believed this was a case of Spirit manifesting in more than one place at the same time. He also had cases of apportation of physical objects outside of the séance room.

The apported Buddha

He recalled one instance, "I was on a unit where a manager had passed away. She was very young. She was the manager of a unit in the hospital. I was talking to one of the charge nurses. She was on one side of a counter of the nurses' station and I was on the other. While we talked something fell right between us.

I asked her, 'Did you see that?'

She acknowledged. I then asked her if someone was behind me and she said, 'You're scaring me.'

I said 'And you're scaring me!'

I picked up a pin from the floor that had the inscription, *Santa loves me*. This was in the middle of April. Neither of us knew where it came from. It was about a week before we were going on a paranormal investigation in a small town outside of Plano. It just so happened that two of the people involved in the investigation were the daughters of the manager who had recently passed. I brought the pin to show them what I had found on their mother's unit.

When I showed it to them, the oldest daughter said, 'That's my mother's pin. Our mother collected pins and that was hers.'

'Where did you get that?' she asked as she examined the pin.

I said, 'I told you, it just dropped out of nowhere.'

I still didn't understand why it showed up saying *Santa loves me*. Well the other daughter's name was Sarah. SLM were the same initials for Sarah, Lara, and Mother. I think it was her way of saying she was with them on this investigation."

Santa loves me pin

Chapter Four: Getting Physical

Spirit continued to tug at Sid during his years at that hospital in Texas. There were many physical phenomena incidents that mostly happened on the unit where the pin had apported. One of the nurses on the unit, Susan was getting more interested in metaphysics. One of her projects was to make stone and crystal bracelets to sell. She was making them for most of the nurses on the unit. Sid was rounding one night. She told him that she wanted to make one for him.

Sid said, "She had a form for me to complete. The form asked questions about my health and spiritual inspirations. I remember complaining that I was always concerned with my heart. I also wanted some protection stones because of all the metaphysical work that I do. Susan was sitting in the breakroom one evening completing my bracelet. I was in the breakroom with her. There were about five other nurses who were sitting around eating their lunch. Susan looked up at me.

She said 'I really need some hematite to complete this bracelet.'

Hematite is a grey magnetic stone that is used for protection amongst other metaphysical properties.

Susan kept saying in a concerning voice, 'I really need some hematite.'

I was opening the door to the breakroom and turned my head saying loudly, 'Susan where in the hell am I going to find hematite, in the middle of the night, at a hospital.'

As I pulled the door open, I realized that there it was on the ground; hematite in a stone form. All six nurses sat there with their mouths open, full of food. I picked the stone up. I handed it to Susan.

I said, 'Here you go! It is the best I could do.'

All were just shocked while nodding their heads. This was only the beginning of the many encounters on this unit.

Some other incidents since the passing of the manager of the unit have been just as remarkable. Multiple nurses had seen a gaseous-like substance travelling down the hall. When it reached the doors that exited the unit the doors would automatically open by themselves. Some of the nurses remarked on a chill of cold air crossing there path as the substance traveled past the nurses' station. Another incident reported multiple times was the phone call between 1 and 2 AM. The phone rang like an outside line would ring. When the phone was picked up there would be no one there. This was the approximate time the manager of the unit would call and check up on them during the night. Some of the nurses would talk into the phone and say some of the things they would have said to the manager. Others would thank her for checking in on them. The manager's presence was a peaceful loving vibe on this unit and the nurses all felt comfortable with her communications."

This is what Spirit does to get your attention. They use things that mean something to you specifically when it's true and pure of heart. It's truly part of your journey in this life. They know what your purpose is in this life. They are only going to expose you to those things that you are ready to handle. If Spirit sees someone at the séance table that is going to be disturbed if someone goes into trance, they are not going to allow it. If something seems really odd to you or really sticks out, take it as a sign and meditate on it.

In late 2013, Sid set out to prepare his own physical séance room. He began training a select group of mediums to create the first physical circle of the Metaphysical Resource Center. The purpose of the group was to conduct experiments in physical mediumship in an attempt to obtain physical phenomena from the other side. I was selected as part of the team.

Chapter Five
Birth of the Séance Room

On December 29, 2013, Sid Patrick, his sisters, Sandy and Deidra, along with five others, gathered at the Metaphysical Resource Center in New Orleans to prepare the new séance room, in the hopes of physical phenomena occurring in the upcoming workshop on physical mediumship.

Sid and his sisters had recently made a trip to a spiritual camp in another state where the two women were introduced to table tipping. Sid had trained in England where table tipping was quite common but his sisters had never before experienced such an event. The group was met by a physical medium who demonstrated a traditional table tipping séance.

Sandy was the most apprehensive. She was skeptical that something of this nature could possibly be real. The physical medium allowed all of them to examine his séance room. They checked the room for trap doors and secret passages. They examined the table for pulleys and strings or anything that may assist in movement of the table. Upon finding nothing questionable about the room, they began the séance. The medium pointed out to them the size of the table's legs.

"You don't want to have one of those land on your foot," he warned, "Make sure you keep your feet under your chair to avoid getting stepped on. If the table gets too close, you can slide your chair back. If your loved one comes through, you can ask yes or no questions. If the answer is no, the table will stop. If the answer is yes, the table will move. Most importantly, do not ask your loved one about anyone else on the other side. If Grandpa is on the table, don't ask him about another loved one. It takes a great deal of effort to come through, so enjoy the visit. It's very disrespectful to ask to speak to someone else. Spirit takes things very literally. If you ask your Grandpa, "Where is Grandma?" he will go look for her. You will lose the connection. Also, no clapping as it breaks up the energy. We will lose the connection. Place your hands lightly on the table. If the table moves away, let it. Don't try to hold on. You'll wind up being pulled off of your chair."

The medium chose where they were to sit. He kept the family members together.

The physical séance is often conducted in complete darkness. Ectoplasm cannot be seen in normal lighting. Sometimes a red light can be added to assist with seeing other physical phenomena. All physical séances begin with the medium saying a prayer of protection over the room. Everyone is envisioned in God's white light for healing and protection. The séance begins with the Lord's Prayer. Songs are then sung to raise the vibration level to allow communication with Spirit. Upbeat, energetic songs work best. The more energy created in the room, the higher the vibration.

Throughout the séance, the table swayed. It then jumped and stood on its side. At one point, the trio's grandmother visited them through the table. Sandy, although skeptical, played along with questions for Grandma. The table even hugged her by pushing up against her. When the session was ending, Sandy said, "I love you, Grandma."

The table stopped abruptly then moved in such a way to cause the legs to squeak. But the message was clear. The table had spoken. It said, "I love you, too."

In that very moment, she experienced what Sid calls *her* "aha" moment. She lost all skepticism. She broke down into a fit of tears. It was at this point that she truly believed that her grandmother had communicated with her. She and her sister vowed to help Sid in his effort to open a local center offering healing table tipping séances to the public. The center first opened in September, 2013. Three months later, the séance room was complete. Next began the tedious process of energizing the

Chapter Five: Birth of the Séance Room

room to open the portal. In addition to the table, the room also contained a medium's cabinet.

The cabinet is the epicenter of energy for the séance room. The cabinet is narrow and high. It is covered with a heavy curtain in the front of it. A medium can be placed inside for the purpose of raising the energy inside, creating a portal through which spirits may enter the séance room. During a table tipping session, a medium may be in the cabinet, but not always.

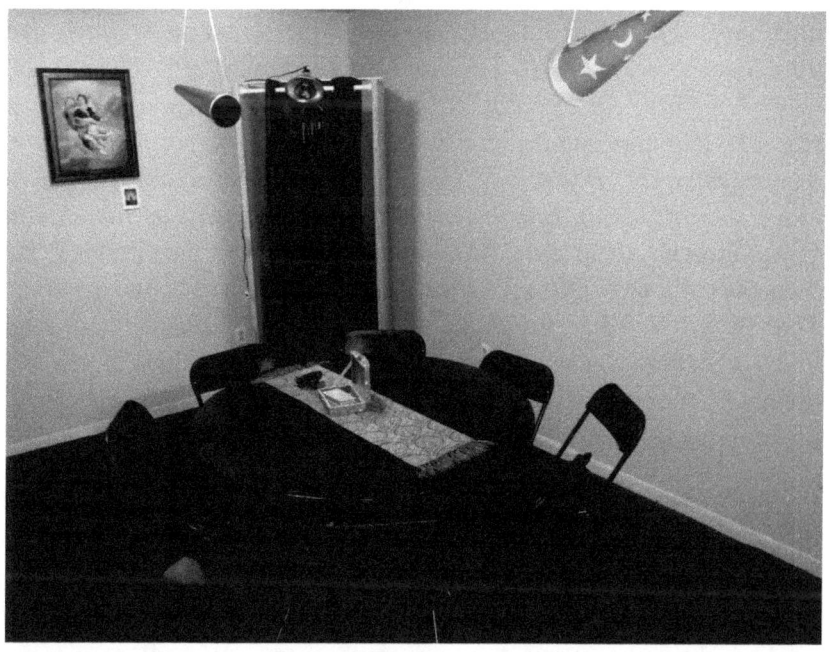

The Séance Room as it looked in October 2014.

Kalila Smith & Sid Patrick

For the first few sessions, Sid and I were joined by other mediums to help prep the table. At least once a week for several weeks, various mediums were brought to the table for one to two hour sessions to energize the table, in the hopes of receiving some sort of physical reaction in the table. We met at the same time each week for the sake of consistency.

Sid said:

Sitting with Spirit is an open invitation to blend our energies. Heaven is paralleled to our world and just as busy. Just as we have jobs and things to do, so do they. You must make an appointment with Spirit. You have to be consistent. The séance room is a place for experimenting with Spirit. Those on the other side are learning what you can handle and how you best relate. Always have an open mind. Don't limit your expectations. If you place limitations on Spirit, they will only take you as far as you have allowed them to. Most importantly, the group must be cohesive. We must all have love and compassion for one another. This is not a place for egos. It is love that connects us with Spirit. If there are negative emotions or motives, Spirit will not connect. If one person has fears or doubts, it will hold the whole group back.

On that cold December night when Sandy and Deidra joined the group like they did in Florida, the conditions became right for physical phenomena to develop. Almost immediately, the table began to vibrate. Several times within the first few minutes, it bucked then the room became very cold. We all saw what appeared to be tiny particles of bright snow floating over the table. Several of us witnessed bright sparks of tiny lights flashing about. I could see shadows darting about behind Sid. We began to sing. We sang old songs such as "I've Been Working on the Railroad" and "Row, Row, Row Your Boat." These types of songs are fast paced. Most people remember the words. It's not so much the words of the song that is important but the participation, as a group, to raise the energy. The point is to get everyone singing and laughing.

Chapter Five: Birth of the Séance Room

The room became even colder. I could feel something touching my legs under the table. I felt the "spider web" type ectoplasm move gently across my face. I sang even louder. Sid moved himself into the cabinet. We continued to sing. The table moved erratically but moved nonetheless. Sid sat quietly in the cabinet in hopes of manifesting ectoplasm. We all watched as we sang with anticipation. But something felt odd to him. His mother's spirit spoke to him instructing him to put Sandy in the cabinet. The two changed places. Once inside the cabinet, she quickly fell into a deep trance state. We continued to sing but the table remained rather sluggish. For some reason unknown to me at the time, I blurted out, "Put in a CD." It was as if some other voice took over and gave instructions.

Someone left the table to turn on the CD player, which still had the CD used in our most recent mental séance. The moment the music came on the table responded by moving, first slowly then speeding up. It vibrated even more. It continued to buck. Soon it was time once again for Stephanie's favorite song to play. As I heard the first few chords, I felt her presence enter the room. I literally felt the energy shift as if she pushed through some sort of membrane. I said, "Here we go."

Soon the table was swaying so fast it was as if it would take flight. I knew my daughter was present. I called out to her. The table pushed up against me hard. I asked questions. In response the table jumped up and down as if it was laughing. This was something new for not only me but for her, too. It was her first attempt at physical manifestation. The table danced in time with the music as she answered a few simple questions. All too soon she was gone as other spirits came to say hello to the group.

Meanwhile, Sandy's breathing became very loud and rhythmic as the room became colder. With each breath, white ectoplasm came from her, filling the cabinet. She did not speak but she moved her hands and arms in various poses. Her facial features seemed to morph into other personas as the spirits shadowed over her face. At one point, she looked as if she was holding an infant to her shoulder. She cradled her arms as if she held a baby. She rocked back and forth with it. We all watched in amazement.

This was a monumental moment. The room was energized and the table moved. We closed the circle. We brought Sandy out from the cabinet then all discussed what we all experienced. She was completely unaware of what had happened to her in the cabinet. Trance mediums never see or hear what they are channeling. The experience is for those outside of the cabinet.

We achieved in a few short months what had taken others years to accomplish. We had a physical séance room that not only had a table that moves, but a cabinet that produced ectoplasm. We fully believed, at this point, that we were not the only ones who wanted this room to come into being, but Spirit wanted it as well. This area needed the healings that would soon take place inside this room. Soon, the general public would be able to experience this life changing event.

As the team continued to prepare the room, the first anniversary of my daughter's death was soon upon me. The year had flown by. No matter how much evidence of an afterlife exists, it never replaces the physical presence of my child in my life. I had kept myself busy as so to not become depressed but now it was inevitable. As the anniversary date approached, I found myself slipping into sadness, even though I tried very hard not to. I sat in my car, parked on the side of the street one evening before work, wondering if I would ever see my child again. I choked back the tears at the thought of never seeing her. I said out loud, "How will I know that I'm ever going to see you again?"

I glanced up just as a car was passing by. The car moved up a few feet and stopped at the intersection. I watched in awe as the car eased up, revealing the only license plate in the state with word "BELIEVE" inscribed on it. I was so stunned that it did not even enter my mind to try to photograph it. In a moment, the car pulled away, as I still sat staring in shock. It was too coincidental to not be a sign from Stephanie. Immediately, I knew that God heard my prayers. He answered them in that very moment.

Chapter Five: Birth of the Séance Room

I shared the experience with Sid, who was then prompted to get glow in the dark bracelets for the séances that read "believe" on them. He gave them to customers as part of the séance experience.

Several weeks later, the center was offering healing table tipping sessions to anyone who wanted them. By then, we had formed our official physical mediumship circle team. My sister-in-law attended one of the very first public sessions. She had gotten some very good messages from my brother from mediums since the previous summer, but I wanted her to experience this physical phenomenon.

As soon as we finished singing, when I introduced myself, the table responded immediately by creaking.

"Is that you, Stephanie?" I asked.

The table stood still, silently. This indicated that it was not Stephanie. I had been getting a lot of communication from her recently. Apparently, she was letting someone else come through for a visit. Since my sister-in-law was present, my first thought was that it was my brother.

"George, is that you?" I asked.

The table literally jumped with joy. Everyone present laughed in delight at the energy he brought to the table.

I asked him, "Where have you been, fishing?"

Apparently, this was correct. The table bounced around as if it was laughing. The table then went to my sister-in-law, pressing up against her firmly.

She exclaimed, "Oh, he's hugging me! I can feel his hug!"

We all encouraged her to talk to him so as not to lose connection. But she was so overwhelmed with emotion, she was unable to think much less speak. The table lifted up onto only one leg and leaned into her even more. Sid put the red light on and held it under the table to show us all how Spirit is able to lift a two hundred pound table and suspend it in midair. My sister-in-law began to cry, saying my brother's name over and over again. The table held still over her as my brother sent her healing love. When Spirit performs a healing like this on a loved one, the person receiving the healing energy may begin to feel a great deal of heat. Simultaneously, the others feel intense cold. Spirit uses energy (heat) in the room, directing that energy to the person being healed. As heat is directed to that one person, others in the group will experience the absence of heat or a cold spot. Most of us were able to remove our hands from the table to demonstrate that it was being held by Spirit. The table stood up by love alone. The table would not lower until he was ready to lower it.

My sister-in-law, like others who have experienced this, knew instinctively that this was indeed the spirit of my brother, her husband. Because we retain our distinct personalities after we cross over, we are easily recognized by our loved ones.

When the healing was over, she told him, "I miss you."

The table creaked, "I miss you too."

The following day was Valentine's Day. It was also another night in the séance room. Prior to the upcoming evening's event, I decided to finally clean my van that had been sitting in my driveway for over a year. There was so much that belonged to Stephanie that I had not been able to clean it. There were the papers from her release from the hospital, still on the seat where they had been placed over a year before. Unable to face taking her things out of the van, it was parked for the past thirteen months.

But now it was time. Tears streamed down my face as I went through each item in the vehicle. When the painful task was complete, I saw something white sticking out from under one of the backseat floor mats. I lifted the mat. I found a small polystyrene foam heart underneath. I had no idea from where it came or how it got there. The only person who ever sat in the third back seat was Stephanie. She often enjoyed lowering the seat in front into a small table for herself. She sometimes coloured on it when we took trips. Then I remembered, "It's Valentine's Day."

Valentine's Day was always something very special to Stephanie. She always loved a good party. In her circles, it was always a day of celebration with music, treats, and colourful Valentine's cards, exchanged amongst friends. My daughter loved to draw and paint. She was extremely artistic. Every year

Chapter Five: Birth of the Séance Room

for Valentine's Day, she would create a handcrafted card especially for me. She drew colourful flowers and stick figures of the two of us, along with our pets. It usually not only expressed her love for me, but always a *thank you* for being her mom. She was the embodiment of unconditional love throughout her entire life. I felt sad that morning missing the Valentine's surprise that I would not get this year. Bittersweet tears flowed down my face as I realized that I held in my hand a gift from my daughter on the other side. It mattered not that I had no explanation how she did it. I knew it was from her. Unbeknownst to me at that time, she had another gift for me; one she would present that evening in the séance room.

That evening, the group gathered again for another session. Every physical medium hopes for more than just table tipping. There are many other physical manifestations that can occur. Séance trumpets (cones) are suspended from the ceiling. They can emit ectoplasm from Spirit sometimes swinging back and forth. Apports such as coins or other objects can appear as a demonstration of Spirit. Voices can manifest out of thin air. But the best hoped-for scenario is a full-bodied apparition to materialize.

During the session, Stephanie came to the table. We felt her as she entered between another medium and me. She was happy and energetic.

I asked, "Is this my baby? Stephanie?"

She communicated to one of the mediums to tell me that she was a "big girl now" and not to worry about her. She swirled the table around and stood it up on one leg.

I asked, "Are you going to send me more butterflies?"

Through one of the mediums she responded, "Let's learn to do something new. Just watch."

Then the table stopped. We all thought she had gone. Sid suggested we sing "You are my sunshine." It was one of Stephanie's favorite songs. As we sang we felt her energy swirling on top of the table. Tiny sparkles of light appeared above the table. She was trying to manifest as an apparition for me. Physical manifestation is not an easy task, but she seemed determined. We continued to sing encouraging her. We sent her love and energy to help her manifest on the physical plane. As the energy increased above the table, the room got significantly colder. Sid and some of the others could see her head forming above the table. All I could see was swirling bright sparkles, like a tiny tornado. Sid instructed everyone to remove their hands from the table except me.

He told me to sit still and not move my hands.

He said, "Do not reach out to her, let her touch you."

Then he instructed her, "Stephanie, show your mom that you're here."

I then felt an icy breeze run across both of my hands. I could feel the cold breeze coming from above the table. I saw tiny sparkles spin rapidly forming a funnel. Then I felt her come close to my face. I felt her kiss my cheek. Then she vanished. I sat sobbing. She had just given me the best Valentine's Day gift anyone could have ever given me. My precious child reached out from the other side and touched me. I wanted to freeze that moment and stay in it forever. But like everything else since her death, it was a fleeting moment. It was one that I will never forget.

Chapter Six
Written in the Stars

The dead not only tell their stories through mediums or signs, but it has now been shown that entire lives and deaths are seen on astrological charts. The souls of those who have passed carry distinct messages to loved ones left here on the physical plane. It is believed by many that all souls know specifically when they will die. Some also believe that astrology could chart the soul's journey and completion of its purpose in this lifetime as well as show a connection to others who were close to them. The natal chart is a sort of blueprint of the soul's purpose that can be decoded to direct individuals toward their true destiny. Many astrologers believe that the soul chooses when they are born and when they die.

Sid had a chart made which showed a definite link between the times of his mother's passing, and his moving forward as a medium. His mother's passing was on Sunday, February 21, 1988, at 5:30 in the morning, in New Orleans, Louisiana. Through messages received from Spirit during channeling sessions and people who have had near death experiences, we know that when we leave this world, we all experience a life review. We are then spiraled upwards to higher planes of existence. We receive a greater understanding of the workings of the other side. The overriding message seems clear: during Sid's mother's passing, she experienced a profound life review, which helped her ascend the spiraling, evolutionary staircase toward a higher plane of existence and a more expansive understanding of *All That Is*. It was at this precise time in Sid's chart that he spiraled up in his own earthly ascension as a psychic and medium. His mother death's was the beginning for his path in the metaphysical.

The astrologer believed that the death of his mother created a catalyst for Sid to begin his own spiritual journey. This is how it happens for many people. So many of us spend our lives looking no further than the physical life we have in front of us. We get caught up in our education, our friends, our family, our careers, and our never ending search for material gratification. Then we lose someone we cannot live without and it forces us to look beyond the physicality of our world. We want to know where our loved one has gone. We need the assurance that we will be reunited with them in another world. For many of us, this changes our course in life and we begin to seek more of a spiritual existence. It was my daughter's death that pushed me to move forward in my own development. As mentioned earlier, many mediums whom I have met over the years claim to have been motivated by the death of someone significant in their lives.

Sid said of his reading, "It was one of the most informative readings I have ever experienced in my thirty plus years in the metaphysical industry. I believe that astrology helps many to understand their soul's purpose. The reading shed light on many of the questions I had, with answers that not only touched my heart, but assisted me in releasing many angers and fears. I was able to go back and compare my deep and recent ancestry with my sister's. This process opened my eyes to the importance of my journey in this life."

Shortly after his mother's death, Sid was invited by a friend to a workshop on psychic/medium work. The metaphysical door was finally opened and he stepped through it.

Interestingly, his chart also showed an odd synchronicity with Hurricane Katrina, seventeen years later.

He explained, "I was working as a nurse at a hospital in New Orleans when Hurricane Katrina struck. For several days, both during and immediately after the storm, I was stuck at the hospital, where I witnessed many patients die, due to inadequate medical care. I also assisted in the evacuation of many others,

Chapter Six: Written in the Stars

most of whom had only their names and addresses in their pockets for identification.

The temperature inside the hospital was sometimes 120 degrees. We became so depleted that some of us eventually resorted to self IV infusions just to keep going. I was finally able to leave the hospital, pack my SUV and head for Plano, Texas, on the Thursday after the hurricane."

Sid felt that Katrina was in some odd way the return of his mother (Catherine, a variation of Katrina) for one final push on his journey. He was forced out of his comfort zone in New Orleans and into Texas for nine years. The number nine coincidently represents an entire cosmic birth or karmic completion cycle. It was there in Plano that he was able to explore and expand upon his mediumistic skills. When his nine year cycle was up, he returned to his old neighborhood in New Orleans to open his metaphysical center.

Sid also had his and his spouse's natal charts compared and their sun signs both went through Plano, TX. This was very significant in their journey for where two suns cross is where a couple will find an energetic connection. This will bring peace and awareness to the couple. This was Sid and his spouse's place of peace and rejuvenation. Their suns cross on the French Riviera but that will ensure a future tale.

In researching my own birth chart along with Stephanie's death chart, the same conclusions were reached. No doubt, this would appear for many who are so connected through a soul family. Soul families share connections from other lifetimes. Not even death can sever some bonds between family members, close friends, or spouses.

We come into this world with purpose, whether we are aware of that purpose or not. The reasons why we are here to begin with remain a mystery, only to be revealed to us at some further awakening of the soul. For some like Sid, the writing on the wall is more obvious. For others, there is more unfolding to take place. We are all on different journeys. Without a doubt, we cross paths with certain people on our soul's paths for specific reasons. We are connected to others who continue to journey with us through many lifetimes. When a loved one dies and we are left to continue this life without them, there is a reason for that as well, even if the reason is unclear.

Stephanie was disabled in this life and many believe that individuals like her are more advanced spiritually than others. Her work here was done. She came to teach the lesson of unconditional love. My lessons continue as I struggle through my life without her. Perhaps part of my purpose is to tell her story in order to help others. Perhaps as my soul evolves, my purpose will become more evident.

One major point that the astrologer made is that I am a walker between worlds. She described my main configuration in my birth chart:

You have a lot of intention with a specific path in this life and not taking any detours on it. You have a lot of focus. You are what I would call a walker between two worlds; someone who lives in this world but one foot firmly in the other world. You live your life in two different worlds simultaneously and fully. You've been doing it for so long, it seems normal to you but it's not normal to most people. You are a bridge, an oracle between two worlds. The path of mediumship and crossing of the threshold between the two worlds is to turn inward so you can be that bridge between the inner and outer. For the purpose of your soul, being introverted is helping you function as a bridge to both worlds.

She then focused on Stephanie's chart:

Stephanie, like you, had what was called a Finger of Destiny which pointed to her ruling planets. It shows affinity and similarity on a soul level with one another. Even though on the outside she appeared to have a disability, there was something else happening on a soul level. I believe that she chose to have Down syndrome in this life, so that she could come into this lifetime and focus inward on what her soul needed to do.

Chapter Six: Written in the Stars

The synastry chart shows the relationship between your birth chart and her crossing over chart. I put these together to see what shows up, and it shows the Finger of Destiny sign. Her south and north node happen to fall exactly on the focal point on your Finger of Destiny, that zero degree crossing over the threshold that created that walker between worlds that I mentioned. South node is an indication of past lives and the North node indicates activation. It is all about karma and past life connections and to have it at that focal point.

There is something really profound and the time of passing was intentionally and activated you to help others with understanding that crossing over process. It couldn't be more karmic and intentional and meaningful for that. It is deepening your capacity as a medium. So it is some kind of activation for you and it is a catalyst. As time goes on, more will be revealed. The message is 'turning inward in order to reveal the full splendor of your soul.'

Months later, I had a different kind of star reading from Jan Dayton in England. Her Soul Plan Reading is based in the ancient Hebrew gematria (numerology system). The reading is obtained from the sound vibration of the original birth name. The frequencies produced are placed around the Star of David in specific positions. Each position represents specific phases of one's life. The downward triangle represents the physical world and relates usually to the first thirty-five years of life. The upward triangle represents the spiritual path of one's life. The intention of the chart is to activate one's soul plan and align oneself with their unique soul's purpose.

Jan says, "Through the universal law of grace, there are many old patterns we can choose to release at this time."

Since my daughter's death, I've often questioned why am I still here? What is my purpose? Because I was her sole caretaker for almost thirty years, I lost not only my child but the purpose for my existence. Since the first portion of the reading related to my earlier years, much of this had already come to pass. I was quite amazed at how accurate this was.

She continued to tell me of a woman who had a child with Down Syndrome whose reading was similar to mine, especially in the healing aspect. Jan had no idea that my daughter had Down Syndrome during her life. The odds are far too high that someone would coincidently mention something like that in a reading. This again, is a form of confirmation that she is receiving messages from Spirit. Like my astrological readings, this star reading indicated that Stephanie's life was in sync with mine for us both to obtain certain spiritual goals.

The deeper meaning here went far beyond just a superficial psychic reading of what may come to pass. This represented a deep karmic bond that she and I shared as only a mother and child could. Each of us was on a spiritual mission to help the other to ascend to the next level, whatever that next level was. We all have a divine purpose. We are all connected to others to help each other on our journeys. Even though my daughter was no longer in this world, she surely continued to walk beside me on this journey we have shared.

At one time or another, we have all questioned our existences. Why am I here? What is my purpose? Why do I have certain connections with some people and not others? What is the meaning of life? Whether you believe that you are here to learn karmic lessons or pay karmic debts, we all have people in our lives with whom we feel connected on a much deeper level than the physical realm. A parent-child relationship is one of the deepest bonds. When our child hurts, we hurt. If we lose a child, it feels as if a part of our soul is ripped out. The connection between the souls of parents and children run deep. I have seen many instances where ancestral spirits return to visit a sitter and know about their lives, and their children's lives, yet the sitter never met them. Our connection to those souls who are familial spirits can never be broken. We retain our connection to our ancestors throughout our entire lives. They are with us when we come into this life. They act as our guides throughout our journey here and await our arrival when we leave this world. We not only often look like an ancestor but can sometimes have a particular personality that is similar to them.

Chapter Six: Written in the Stars

No matter what the purpose, the lesson is clear, love never dies. Connections with our loved ones continue on the other side. The secrets of the universe and eternity are written in the stars like a celestial map. If you learn to read the map properly, the soul's destiny will become apparent.

Chapter Seven
Altered States

Trance mediumship is one of the more intense forms of physical mediumship. The *medium's cabinet* plays an important role for the trance medium. Trance mediums will not only have spirits overshadow them, but also channel them. They speak directly through the medium.

The medium must be induced into an altered state of consciousness allowing Spirit to take control. The deeper the trance, the more Spirit can overshadow and possibly even channel through a medium. Going into trance is similar to being hypnotized. It requires only the ability to relax deeply and trust Spirit. The difference is with hypnosis, the client is fully aware of what is taking place. When a medium is overshadowed by an entity, he/she is not aware of what is happening. As with other forms of mediumship, Spirit decides what takes place in the cabinet. One of the first changes that are noticed is that the medium's breathing slows down, indicating a relaxed, altered state.

The temperature in the cabinet lowers considerably. Many mediums report becoming cold when they first go into trance. The others in the circle send love and energy to the cabinet to assist the one in trance receiving Spirit. Many of those in the room can see not only the white, misty ectoplasm appearing but some see the shadows or images when they step into the cabinet to overshadow the medium. In many sessions, we could see the ectoplasm and tiny, bright sparkles pouring into the cabinet from directly above it. The small enclosed cabinet stores the energy and becomes a portal or doorway between the two worlds.

Sid in the Medium's Cabinet

As overshadowing occurs, onlookers see the face of the medium change. This process is often called *transfiguration*. Not only the features change but hair gets longer or shorter, facial hair can appear, and the medium may appear older or younger. The mouth may move as if it is attempting to speak. Often times, even though the eyes of the medium are closed, what resembles doll eyes appear on the eyelids.

One medium in our group, Silvia, came into the program already channeling her grandmother through automatic writing. She writes in Portuguese, as her grandmother did not know English. Silvia seemed prone to enter into a trance state. She

Chapter Seven: Altered States

was so sensitive that when she barely touched the table, it began to move. She was an open channel to the other side.

Silvia was one of the first to experience the cabinet. She soon channeled a young woman, who called herself Laura. She claimed to be the spirit of a nineteen-year-old young woman who died in a car crash sometime in the 1970s in the New Orleans area. She validated this information by giving details of what the city looked like at that time. She described local attractions to the area. She also described the trees found commonly in the nearby swamplands on the outskirts of the city. Laura was excited to be able to physically speak through Silvia because during her life, Laura was a deaf mute. Much of Laura's physical life was no longer a memory for her. This lends itself to the theory that we forget details of our lives once we cross over similarly as we forget where we were before coming into this incarnation. Laura was thrilled to be able to physically speak and hear. She also indicated that she had been studying Silvia for some time.

Laura complained that Silvia was not paying attention to the signs. She said, "I try to get this girl to buy red roses like her grandmother likes. She looks at them but won't buy them." Laura told the group that she watched Silvia in her house. She admitted to playing a joke on her by planting a single sunflower seed in her garden.

Laura told the group that there were many spirits on the other side who wanted to communicate. She said, "You should see them, all lined up here. It is so unorganized! We need to get organized here, it's very messy!"

Laura pointed up to the ceiling, she asked, "Can you see the bright light there?"

Laura explained that she was able to channel through Silvia because of an agreement with Silvia's grandmother. She explained that the grandmother was a healer on the other side, just as she had been here on earth. She knew many people and had befriended Laura. She agreed to allow Laura to speak through Silvia so she could experience speaking.

During one of Silvia's experiences in the cabinet, not only did her face change but so did her entire persona. She changed posture, taking on a more masculine position with her arm on her knee. She dropped her head and when she lifted it, she appeared completely different, with a serious look on her face. She looked around as though she had no idea where she was. A deep voice emitted from her throat, "Where am I?"

Sid welcomed him, "What is your name, Spirit?"

"I am Gary," he answered.

"Welcome, Gary," Sid said.

I sat there, stunned, staring blankly at him, unable to speak. I knew him in life for over twenty years. He left this world suddenly, exactly eight months before my daughter. He had communicated during numerous readings from mental mediums as well as direct contact to me through dreams. Now, he sat before me inside the body of a medium, having no clue as to what had happened. He looked directly at me.

"Oh my God!" he exclaimed.

I said nothing. He continued to repeat it over and over again. Meanwhile, I sat there, staring at him, practically falling off of the chair with shock. Then he got very quiet. He leaned forward.

"I remember you," he said.

After a brief chat to get him accustomed to his surroundings, he described his life to the group. He remained a bit unsure of how he came through but he was pleased that it happened. His visit was not very long but he asked if he could come back sometime. We all agreed that he was welcome to return any time. She later channeled a female singer who could not give a name but was delighted to share her song. Silvia is not a singer so the fact that this beautiful singing voice exuded from her was confirmation alone.

When I got into the cabinet, I went into a trance state more easily than I had expected. I could feel myself in the cabinet but at the same time, traveling to other places. The cabinet became very cold. I heard the group say that they could see a warrior over me, specifically a Samurai warrior. I was surrounded by a lot of bright white ectoplasm, as if I was inside of a cloud. I

Chapter Seven: Altered States

moved very rapidly into a scene. I found myself sitting on the ground. I was dressed as a Native American woman surrounded by other Native women who were similarly dressed. There was a Native man standing beside me singing and chanting. He wore a feather in his hair that was pointed down. I felt as if he was a medicine man. I could smell sweet grass burning. I knew instinctively that I was participating in some sort of purification ritual.

I found myself on a large plain with buffalo in the background. The other part of me could still feel being inside the cabinet. I was bilocating. I heard someone in the séance room say that they could see the Native American's face overshadow mine.

I was then quickly teleported to a jungle that looked like what I'd seen in Central America and Mexico. It felt as if I was literally sucked out of one scene as if in a vacuum, then hurled into another. Yet, I could still feel my presence in the cabinet at the same time.

A huge stone temple stood in front of me. There were mountains in the background. I could hear running water. I somehow knew that a river and waterfall were nearby. The nearby trees were covered by thick vines. Little monkeys chattered about. Amidst this beautiful jungle scene, I was surrounded by jaguars, both spotted and black ones. I felt no fear. I came face to face with a jaguar, as if the animal and I were one. I could hear the other mediums in the room say that they could see both the monkey and the jaguar shadow my face.

During my experience in the cabinet, I saw bright white lights and a lot of blinking coloured lights around me. When I came back to full awareness, several mediums saw me leave my body and return.

I later consulted with my friend, who is a member of the Choctaw tribe. He went into a trance and channeled a message for me.

He said, "What is happening here is more involved than what you people are aware of at this time."

He assured me that it would happen again and that more would be revealed.

What was most interesting was that the second scene looked very much like some of the Mayan ruins I had seen. I was planning an excursion to the area in October, while on a cruise, and planned to visit some ruins. I had also recently had a past life chart done, and one of my past life lines on the chart fell directly through Merida, Mexico, where I would be in October. Many fellow psychic/mediums felt that I would experience some spiritual awakening during my visit.

Validation of my trance experiences came to me when I traveled to the ruins of Dzibilchaltun, just outside of Merida, Mexico. Dzibilchaltun is a small Mayan village that was inhabited until the Spanish invasion. In the middle of the village sit the remnants of one of the first Catholic churches alongside Mayan structures.

Entering the property felt like stepping back in time. We walked down the pathway through the jungle to the large open village. I felt a sense of peace as I stepped onto the sacred land. A beautiful jungle surrounded the open village. Directly in front of us was the burial ground of those who once lived here. Huge white and yellow butterflies flew about the area. To the right, was their village, the place where they lived, worked, and worshipped. To the left sat a magnificent structure named the Temple of the Seven Dolls. When the temple was rediscovered in the 1950s, seven small sculpted dolls were found inside. The opening of the temple is in direct alignment with rising sun during the spring and fall equinoxes. This was an important time for planting and harvesting for the Mayans. The amazing thing about the temple was that I had envisioned it during my sessions in a trance state in the cabinet. In the vision, there was more jungle indicating that my vision of the area was from an earlier time. The entire meaning of my vision was still unclear. I felt oneness with the land, and with the temple. No doubt to fully understand my connection would require more experiments in the cabinet.

Chapter Seven: Altered States

Sid became entranced with cabinet work during one of his visits to Arthur Findlay College in England. One of the instructors was conducting an exercise in energy. During this exercise, the students were asked to move the energy around a circle and create a vortex.

Sid told me of his first experience:

The instructor told the class that if anyone during the exercise felt compelled to say something, he should say it.

Most of the students were giving messages of love and world peace. While sitting in that circle, I felt a force pushing on me almost taking me off of my chair. Then without effort, my mouth opened and I said, "Harry, get the damned flowers off of the bed."

Everybody stopped and looked at me as if I were crazy. I had a vision of someone coming home, and all of these flowers spread over a bed. I do not know if this had a connection with the medium, but I do know that after the exercise, I was told by this instructor that I had physical mediumship capabilities and I should pursue that journey. After that event, I had to return to my room because the exercise left me feeling nauseated.

On the following evening, I attended a séance which included some time in the cabinet. Everyone was searched prior to entering the room. Two balls were thrown and those who caught them were allowed to check the room to verify that nothing was rigged. The attending medium was then handcuffed to his chair inside the cabinet. Two people sat next to the cabinet to ensure that nothing was manipulated by the medium. The rest of the group held hands. Once the energy was raised, musical instruments that were set on the floor began to play and fly around the room. Two trumpets lifted and crossed each other in midair. Even though it was dark, these instruments were illuminated as to be witnessed by those present. There was also a ball that rolled across the room and hit me. I could feel the spirit of a young child who touched my knee as he came for the ball.

During this kind of physical demonstration of Spirit, it is important for those in the circle to keep holding hands. This is strictly for the protection of the medium, while he/she is producing ectoplasm. At one point, someone broke the connection by dropping their hand and the spirit that was being channeled by the medium actually stopped the session until the connection was made again. It was so dark in that room; there was no way for the medium to physically see that he had dropped his hand. This was pretty amazing that this guide could actually see or sense what was going on at the séance.

This medium was handcuffed inside of the cabinet. Everyone in the room witnessed the cabinet, levitating over their heads and moving to the other side of the room. When the lights came back on, not only had the cabinet moved over us to the side, but all of the chairs in the room were stacked on top of one another, blocking him inside. He had literally transported above the audience. Later, I witnessed Spirit picking up a bottle of water then opening it and pouring it into a glass using only ectoplasm. Not one drop spilled.

I had the opportunity to sit in trance myself. As I was sitting in that chair, I felt a very cold wind wrapping around my head. I felt as if spider webs were wrapping across my face. I could feel myself stepping back then seeing myself from behind. I had completely left my body! As I did this, I ran across one of my guides. This guy has been with me since I was a very young child. He had shown me things but had never spoken to me. I witnessed him step over me and sit directly on top of my body, still seated in the chair. While my hands were in my lap, I watched him raise one of his hands and wave at the others who were present.

When I was brought back to my body and out of trance, I was told what the others had witnessed. They saw me age and grow a beard. They all witnessed a hand raising and waving to them. That was my first physical experience of being overshadowed by Spirit. This was the key step in leading me down the path of physical mediumship.

Everyone's experience with trance work is different. Each medium has their own guides and masters with whom they

Chapter Seven: Altered States

connect. In all instances, the medium is in an altered state of consciousness and has minimal recollection of what occurred during a channeling session. In a group setting, the group witnesses what Spirit displays, then, the medium is informed afterwards what took place. Many of the more adept trance mediums connect with higher masters to bring messages to individuals to help guide them on their own paths or help them heal from grief by connecting them to a departed loved one. In every instance, the intent is to offer what is in that person's best interest.

The main concern, when working with trance, is that the medium is always safe. There should always be another medium in attendance that is not in a trance state. If not a medium, then it should be someone who is able to control the situation during the trance state. This person should also be able to bring the medium back into a fully conscious state.

It is also imperative that the room be properly prepared before the session. This will be discussed at length in a later chapter. Additionally, it should be insured that no one will abruptly awaken or jolt the medium back to their fully conscious state.

Any séance, particularly where trance is involved should be approached with the utmost respect. Always the main concern is for the medium's safety.

Chapter Eight
Walkers Between Worlds

The term *walkers between worlds* is often used when referencing shamans who use meditation and herbs to alter their consciousness and travel outside of their bodies into other dimensions. These individuals can transport themselves to the past or future. Indigenous spiritual leaders were the early mediums. Many ancient religious paths tell of medicine men engaging in astral projection to other dimensions and shape shifting. They commonly brought back messages from the spirit world or healings for others.

Death is not seen as an ending in these traditions. It is a continuation of the soul's journey through many worlds. Our loved ones are believed to be with us, but in Spirit. Those who no longer live in the physical body are believed to have great knowledge and are consulted for their wisdom and advice. Ancestors long gone from this world continue to work on our behalf on the other side. The dead are not worshipped but honored and remembered every day. They are contacted just as we would pick up the telephone and call a friend.

It is a widely held belief that children see into both worlds. Young children and babies who have just come into this physical existence see, hear, and experience spirits in a way that older people do not. Have you ever watched a little baby play alone? The infant will look about and smile at what seems like nothing there. Just as animals have a keen sixth sense, so do babies.

There have been numerous recent reports of young children remembering their past lives. One young boy actually remembered dates, names of people he knew, and the name of the ship on which he fought in World War II. I have come across many people who heard and saw spirits as a child but at a certain point in their development, the ability ceased.

People like my daughter, who are born mentally challenged, remain like children. Without a doubt, throughout my daughter's lifetime, she had a special connection with spirits and constantly had interactions with them. I believe that special people come into this world to bring unconditional love. They connect with realms that are unseen to the rest of us. Stephanie constantly chattered with invisible friends in her room. Sometimes, I would hear her talk to them while she was playing video games or watching movies. In her final months, she had begun to stay up until odd hours. Sometimes I would wake up in the early morning and find her colouring at the kitchen table and talking to someone. Any time that I would inquire about her visitors, she would quickly dismiss it.

Sid said, "Children are in very early stages of brain development. This comes before we are conditioned to think about life's structure, before we get too brainwashed by society by how things have to be. If you are referring to special kids, the brain operates on energy so anything that has a brain difference would definitely link them to the right side of their brain to help them use the Clairs with more efficiency."

Several months after my daughter's death in 2013, a friend's son, who was also special needs, began asking to speak to me. He told his mother that he wanted to discuss spirits and that I would understand. Having so much on my plate at the time and difficulty dealing with my loss, I did not readily respond to his request. Then one night, my daughter appeared in a dream instructing me to listen to what he had to say to me. She said it would help me understand what she and other special need children experienced on the other side.

Mark is an eighteen-year-old young man with a congenital condition that has left him with developmental disabilities. He has spoken directly to spirits his entire life and now felt prompted to share his experiences with me. I conducted an interview with him that was quite amazing.

Chapter Eight: Walkers Between Worlds

Q: *Tell me about what you see when you see spirits.*

A: *I can see earthbound spirits before and after death.*

Q: *Can you explain that a bit more, please? What do you mean before and after death?*

A: *I can see it in my mind, somehow. I can see the spirits like they were before they died and after they died. I see them sometimes like people in front of me or sometimes like pictures in my mind. I can see my Nana. She looked the same like before she died.*

Q: *You have been asking to see me for quite a while. What prompted you to want this interview?*

A: *I just knew you would be interested.*

Q: *Do you have instances where you are out of your body?*

A: *Yes. I can feel myself walking around but I cannot see everything.*

Q: *How do you interpret spirits? Do you see them, feel them, and hear them?*

A: *I can feel if it's a man or a woman or a child or animal. My back gets cold when I see a spirit of a person, an angel or a ghost. If I see a demon, my back gets red and hot. If you have a demon, you can get a box with mirrors and trap them inside their own energy and they cannot get out.*

Q: *Where do they come from?*

A: *They come from the portal. Someone can have a portal in their house for spirits and not even know it's there.*

Q: *Can you explain what a portal is?*

A: *A portal is a doorway from their world to our world. This means they can travel from there to here. The portals exist but no one can see them. The portals are hidden. The portal is in my closet. Never remodel a closet. You can release spirits that way and it might be something you can't control.*

A medium's cabinet is nothing more than a small closet where a portal is created. This is done by raising the energy in a very small space. Sid had demonstrated that portals were often in closets in several haunted locations. By using dowsing rods, he could pinpoint the location of portals. He had even videotaped orbs coming through one portal in a closet then exiting through another. This validated what Mark was explaining to me.

Q: *Does your Nana come through the portal? Where does she come from?*

A: *Yes, but she comes from Heaven's Gate. The Heaven's Gate is a place where spirits go and they can travel back and forth. Bad spirits do not go there. There is also an outpost and she can see them.*

Q: *You mentioned angels. Do you see angels? What is your interpretation of angels?*

A: *Angels can have wings or they can walk. I've seen quite a few. One had a hood on its head that looked like it was going to a wedding. Angels can be a woman or a man. I can also see people from past time experiences.*

It should be noted that even though many people believe that angels have no gender, those who have channeled from the other side portray it differently. They do mention gender. In fact, in the Old Testament, it was fallen angels who mated with the

Chapter Eight: Walkers Between Worlds

daughters of man, creating the giants. In many ancient cultures, similar beings are described as having specific gender.

Q: *What does that mean?*

A: *Past time experiences are when you see things that happened a long time ago. I can see a house like it looked a long time ago.*

Q: *What do you tell spirits when they come through to you?*

A: *I tell them, "It's okay, I can see you. You're not alone. I can see you and I can help you."*

Q: *How do you help them?*

A: *I tell them to find the light and go to the light. If they don't see it then it means that there is something they need to do before they can go into it. Usually, if they cannot go into the light that means they have unfinished business here and they have to take care of that before they can go. Then there's also the shadow spirits.*

Q: *Tell me about the shadow spirits.*

A: *Shadow spirits are evil spirits. They drag down good spirits and try to make them bad. They try to keep them from going through the light. The shadow spirits are afraid of the light. The light burns their eyes. They don't want to leave earth.*

Q: *Are the shadows the same as a demon?*

A: *No, they are different. They are not as evil but they are trouble. They can change someone's whole future.*

Q: *So what is your purpose in this life?*

A: *I believe I was given a gift to help people who die to find the light before the shadow spirits get to them.*

During one of Silvia's channeling sessions, a visiting spirit, Laura, was asked if she saw angels. She responded that she did not see many of them where she was. She said they lived on another level. Then she said, "Your daughter hangs out with angels. She is on a different level than I am. She is around angels more than the rest of us."

This came as no surprise to me. Stephanie was always someone who was not truly of this world. Several times that she has channeled through a medium, she refers to her death as "going home." Many others consider people like Stephanie as very special spirits with very special missions in this life. They teach us how to be selfless. They teach the true meaning of Divine love to those of us who might otherwise miss the message. I was fortunate enough to be blessed with her as my daughter. The almost thirty years that I spent caring for her were the best years of my life.

Shortly after she left this world, an elder in Santeria sent a message to me telling me that normally we pray for a spirit of the deceased so it may ascend to its highest potential. She explained that we need not do that for Stephanie because she was already ascended throughout her entire life.

A very good friend of mine has a sixteen-year-old daughter who suffers from cerebral palsy. Despite the fact that this girl cannot walk, nor talk, nor even lift her arms from her sides, when she is brought into a church service, her entire demeanor changes. She becomes more alert the moment the singing commences. She no longer gazes vaguely past everything but focuses intently at one particular corner of the church. She laughs and tries to lift her arms up as if reaching out for someone. She vocalizes as though she is trying to sing. She sees someone there that the rest of us do not.

Whether these kids are seeing angels or perhaps loved ones who have passed before them is unknown. All that is known is that these special children have a connection that we do not. We

Chapter Eight: Walkers Between Worlds

have to work to get even a small glimpse of what they see and hear clearly. They give us further validation that there is something out there beyond this physical world that we call life.

Many people develop dementia in their older years. The memory declines. Patients often forget people in their life. Interestingly however, often times, these people who struggle with dementia do remember those from their distant past. Many Alzheimer's patients tell loved ones of their encounters with other family members who have crossed over long ago. I have even had instances where during a session with a sitter, I pick up on the patient who is still alive physically but riddled with Alzheimer's or some other form of dementia. Their spirits sometimes can have the same feel of one who has crossed over into the spirit world.

People suffering from these diseases, or those who are close to crossing over, such as those in their final days of battling cancer, will often leave their dying bodies only to return periodically. One client seemed shocked at first when I explained that her mother was coming through because as she explained, her mother was alive. I felt very embarrassed that I not only told her that her mother had stepped up but was showing me that she was enjoying dancing. I asked her if her mother had some form of dementia. She acknowledged that she did. I then asked her if her mother ever talked about taking trips outside of her body. She again responded affirmatively, telling me that she spoke of visits with other family members who were deceased. When I told her about seeing her mother dancing, she informed me that her mother mentioned an uncle and that the two of them liked to dance in their younger days. I said, "They still do."

Without a doubt, children like my daughter and those outlined here, see our world through different eyes. Even if they may seem to be disabled, what they lack, they make up for with their attunement to nature and the spirit world. They are very special people who give gifts to every life they touch. Their message is simple: love unconditionally. Trust your senses. In many ways, they are far more advanced than we could ever possibly be in this lifetime.

Chapter Nine
The Healers

Physical mediumship has many faces. Trance mediumship includes trance healers. A medical intuitive is someone who intuitively senses illness in others. Sid is a medical intuitive as is my friend, Phillip. When Phillip first read my palm many years ago, he predicted a serious health issue.

"You are going to have a major setback due to illness in your early fifties," he told me.

"Great," I said, trying to maintain my composure.

"Who tells somebody this?" I thought to myself.

At the time, barely knowing Phillip, the last thing I wanted to hear was that something bad was going to happen. I walked away from that reading hoping that he was wrong. For many years, I worried that at some point, I would have a stroke or heart attack. My fears focused mainly on the pain that would be involved. I also worried about being incapacitated and needing rehabilitation. This knowledge of an impending illness was quite fretful for me. It was like a dark cloud that loomed over me. After almost a decade had gone by, however, I had all but forgotten the prophecy and had become very good friends with Phillip. He too, had forgotten his prediction.

Then at the age of fifty-one, I developed several uterine fibroid tumors. I suffered for two years with massive hemorrhaging and pain. When hormone therapy no longer controlled the bleeding and pain, it became necessary to get a full hysterectomy.

Due to the uncertainty of what else might have been ailing me, the surgery required cutting me from hip bone to hip bone. I was literally cut in half and sewn back together. During the surgery, my bladder was accidently cut, prolonging the healing process. It would be many months before I would recover fully. By that time, I had completely put Phillip's prediction out of my head. Then one day, we were having wine together and he remembered the reading.

"You know, I think that surgery you had was the illness I saw coming many years ago. It finally makes sense," he said. "Oh wow, I had forgotten all about that prediction," I said.

We both got a good laugh reminiscing about our first meeting through that palm reading session.

It was also through a psychic that I was alerted to seek a physician for serious metabolic imbalance. Freddie Rivera is a medical intuitive in addition to being a psychic/medium. After Freddie had done such a phenomenal job contacting Stephanie and my parents on the other side, I decided to contact him for a regular psychic reading. Freddie psychically scanned my entire body during a phone reading. He explained to me that when he scanned, it was as if he had a giant laser that began at the head of the client then slowly moved down stopping along the way at points of distress or possible illness. Because he does this intuitively, he can even conduct a body scan long distance.

In his book, *The Shining Within Me*, Freddie explained how this worked for him during readings:

At one point during the reading, I felt compelled to close my eyes. When I closed my eyes, I began to see the outline of a woman's body. Then the colourful aura followed as it did in my meditation...I realized that I was seeing the body of the woman for whom I was reading in my mind's eye. Not only that, I began to see a dark spot around her kidney area. (Rivera, 165)

Freddie asked the woman if she had a problem with her kidneys and much to his surprise she revealed to him that she not only had kidney disease but was in need of a transplant. This is how he realized that he was a medical intuitive. He could see illnesses in others through his mind's eye rather than direct sight.

Chapter Nine: The Healers

He visualized my body scan during a phone reading just as he had conducted my mediumship session. After he concluded my reading he asked me if I would like to receive a medical scan. I agreed to it. He immediately noted my sinus condition and then some dental work that I had recently done. He then proceeded to psychically scan down my neck and each arm.

"Do you have carpal tunnel or some sort of injury in your wrists?" he asked.

Of course I did. As a writer, I am constantly overworking my fingers, hands, and wrists. I have struggled with symptoms of carpal tunnel for many years. After that, he focused his intent on my upper back. He noted the misalignment I had in my spine. He knew about the fact that sometimes my arms became numb due to the nerve compression there. He scanned down my legs and mentioned my low back and knee problems.

When he completed the scan, Freddie suggested I have some diagnostic tests conducted. He mentioned that I might have something going on with my pancreas. He asked if I was diabetic. My mother had suffered with diabetes her entire life. Although I had not developed it, I was certainly at risk. Fortunately, my condition had not exacerbated into full blown diabetes. My physician determined that I had a pre-diabetic condition called *metabolic disorder,* which included insulin resistance. My body was producing more insulin than needed, causing a myriad of symptoms. Freddie's psychic medical analysis prompted me to consult a doctor before my body progressed into a fully diabetic state.

Freddie wrote:

When I run my hand over an area of a person's body, I am able to detect trouble areas where illness could or has developed. Usually, chakra areas on the body are cold when the chakra is unhealthy or needs to be opened, cleared, or aligned. (Rivera, 166)

A trance healer is a bit different from a medical intuitive. The trance healer goes into an altered state of consciousness as

Spirit steps into the medium, using him/her as a tool to channel healing energy to the client. A good example of this is Reiki. The practitioner uses the manipulation of energy to break up blockages of energy and relieve pain and facilitate healing to take place. The energy is coming from the Divine rather than the practitioner using their energy. As with mental mediumship, the practitioner is merely the tube or vehicle for channeling the healing energy to the patient.

I have used Reiki for many years using direct contact with my hands while conducting a healing session. During the healing, my hands usually become very hot. I have broken out in a heavy sweat just from pulling heat from another while conducting a healing session. During a session, my hands will instinctively go to the areas of the person's body that are in pain or inflamed. I can feel the pain from their body going through my hands and sometimes up my arms. The worse the pain, the more intense feeling I will get when I work on the individual.

I also incorporate Qi Gong, another type of Asian energy healing, to move stagnate or blocked energy in a person's body in order to facilitate healing. During a session, the Reiki or Qi Gong practitioner must maintain a light trance state and not allow thoughts or distractions to take away from the session. The practitioner is used as a tube by the universal energy of God to connect Divine healing energy. Usually the client also becomes very relaxed, even drowsy during a session. Both Reiki and Qi Gong forms of energy healing can be done direct on an individual or long distance. All that is required is a willingness to receive the healing energy in order for it to work. Since everything physical including disease happens first on an energetic level, healings as well take place on the energetic plane then affect the physical body.

Early Chinese medicine and most tribal medicine maintain that all disease begins with dysfunction on the energetic level or from a disconnection from the Divine. Early healers treated not only the body but the spirit of those who were ill. The basis of acupuncture is treating the energy meridians which lie deep inside the body, invisible to the eye. These energy points carry

Chapter Nine: The Healers

life force energy throughout the body. When in balance, the body remains healthy. When there is a blockage of energy caused by a physical injury or emotional distress, the body becomes pain ridden and sick. The body heals by keeping the energy moving.

Other forms of trance healing involve an actual healing entity stepping into the medium and conducting the healing. One trance healer at the metaphysical center worked on my neck to attempt to relieve a pulled muscle. I sat with my eyes closed and he placed his hands gently on my neck. I could feel heat emanating from his hands. My shoulders dropped as stress released from them. I could feel his hands slowly moving my neck from side to side then left to right. As I felt him work on me, I became aware of someone in front of me as well. I opened one eye to see who had walked up and was shocked to see the person whom I thought was behind me. I still could feel his hands on my neck! Others in the room claimed to actually see the figure of a spirit working on my body.

Energy healer Georgina Regan is famous worldwide for her unique healing abilities that she calls "Subtle Energies Catalyst." On her website (www.georginaregan.com), it is stated that scientific tests concluded that she "could produce [and sustain] an electrical current through her hands that could be measured, even though she was not touching the measuring instrument."

Georgina describes her treatments as a method that may "remove blockages, whether they are physical, mental, emotional or spiritual so that the energy flows unimpeded throughout the whole system into the cells, bringing about greater harmony and balance, with great reduction in anxiety, as healing takes place by virtue of the additional strength and energy received."

During her visit to New Orleans, I decided to arrange a healing session with her to address my lower back. I was suffering with intense pain and numbness in my back, left hip, and down my left leg to such a point I had to use a cane to walk.

During the first portion of her session, I felt her standing behind me and could feel her hands working around my head and neck. My hair stood on end as if there was electricity emitting from her hands. At some point, I felt as if her hands were on each side of my head. I felt a gentle positioning of my neck, moving it from side to side and then left and right. I later commented to her that the way she moved my neck was very helpful. She informed that at no time did she physically touch me or move my head.

It was the second portion of the session that really amazed me. She had me lie face down on a massage table. She placed her index fingers on two pressure points along what is called the gall bladder meridian in acupressure (the lateral side of the leg). I felt a second pair of hands also with one finger along the same meridian in between her hands. She was the only other person in the room besides me, yet, there were two sets of hands on me.

She removed her hands and moved around to the front of the table by my head. I could still feel the second pair of hands working on my lower extremities. An unseen being then pulled on my left leg at the ankle creating traction. I felt my left hip loosen and my left leg lengthen. I then felt my entire hip girdle straighten out.

I received another trance healing session a few months later from Lana Davis Johnson of Dallas, Texas. Lana works by going into a deep trance and laying hands on the client. During my session with her, she sat in trance as she placed her hands on my head allowing Spirit to work through her. Although my eyes were closed, I saw a bright white light. There appeared in the light three beings that stood over me. I could see only their outlines; no facial features were visible to me. It was extremely comforting and peaceful as these Angelic beings sent warm energy all over my body. I felt every muscle release, one by one from the top of my head to my toes. The session seemed to be only several minutes long but when it had ended, the clock as well as others in the training session, showed it had been a half hour.

Lana then instructed me to not drink alcohol for twenty-one days as the Angels would continue to work on healing my body. Over the following weeks, I felt stronger and had less pain.

Chapter Nine: The Healers

The power of the Divine working through us to heal is real. Every day that I walk along on this journey I experience more proof of how powerful Spirit really is.

Healings can be physical, mental, or emotional. Spirit is limitless. Whenever someone begins to work with Spirit on any level, changes take place in that individual. Once the door is opened to the spirit world, one begins to evolve. This transformation will continue as long as the individual will allow it to take place. Spirit will allow us to grow as far as we can or will accept.

Old repressed emotions will emerge and be purged as the individual moves further along their path of evolution. Some people become afraid of such changes. This might create a setback in their growth. Once that person is aware that this purging is necessary to move forward, the process becomes easier. When we flow with Spirit on our true paths, everything around us and within us flows as well. When we grow spiritually, we also grow emotionally. Great healings can take place on all levels.

Chapter Ten
Entranced

Some people are simply more open than others. Spirit blends with the path of least resistance. During one table tipping session, Daphne was seated outside of the circle in one corner. During the session, we sang in total darkness and became aware of a knocking sound coming from the corner where she was seated. This had been an extremely intense session, as both of Sid's grandfathers had come through. One was celebrating his birthday. We had just sung happy birthday to him. We called out to Daphne, but she didn't respond. When we turned the red light on, she was in a trance state and was rocking in the chair, unresponsive. However, the problem was that Daphne had never channeled before. Spirit was attempting to speak through her, but all that could be accomplished was the repetitive rocking. As Sid brought Daphne back up from her trance, another medium had also gone into a deep trance state. She began to gasp and cough violently. As she struggled to catch her breath, a deep, gravelly voice of an older woman spoke through her. She raised her right hand as she spoke, her fingers in a V shape as if something was perched between them.

"What about me?" said a voice coming from the medium.

Sid immediately recognized the spirit of his grandmother. She, too, had recently celebrated a birthday. She had become a bit jealous that his grandfathers were getting all the attention. Sid informed us that she had been a heavy smoker throughout her life and, in her later years, had a rough voice because of it.

Silvia was so susceptible to trance that she would go under even when someone else was in the cabinet. During one session, it was Missy's turn to be in the cabinet. Although Spirit did not speak through Missy, she still went into trance quite easily and could leave her body and walk around the room. That in itself was quite a talent. She was sitting in the cabinet and we were listening to music to raise the vibration in the room when suddenly, Silvia began swinging her arms around as if dancing in her chair. Sid was working in the hospital that evening, so we did not have the advantage of his expertise when the course of the evening changed as it did. I could see a female shadow figure in the left corner of the room. Silvia grabbed my arm and pulled me. Then her mouth began to move. Her face contorted and her head jerked as she tried to speak. I could tell that it would not be Laura channeling through her this time. Something new was about to happen.

All of a sudden Silvia opened her mouth and shouted, "Mom!"

It was Stephanie. She was channeling through Silvia. I sat in utter shock as she continued to pull on my arm.

"Mom, I can feel you!" she exclaimed.

By now we were both crying. I held her hand as she squeezed me tightly. I wanted to reach out and hug but was not sure if that would be a good idea. I maintained my composure and she spoke to me.

"You did it, Sweetheart," I told her.

"Mom, I can feel your arm," she cried.

"I know, baby. This is wonderful," I assured her.

Like with the table, Spirit can only manifest for a short time, especially in a case where both the spirit and medium are new to the situation. She soon said good-bye and left her channel.

When Silvia came up out of the trance, she was surprised by what had taken place. Meanwhile, Missy had watched the whole thing from the corner of the room. Even though her body was sitting in the cabinet she was the shadow I saw move into the corner. She saw Stephanie overshadow Silvia. When Stephanie left, she looked at Missy and told her that she would return. Missy also gave me a message.

Chapter Ten: Entranced

She told me, "Stephanie said that you have to go inside of yourself to find your purpose now. She also said, 'Tell my mom, I'm all grown up now."

Silvia and I agreed that if Stephanie did return that it would be alright for me to hug her. Stephanie died suddenly and it was quite a shock for me. There was no time for mental preparations or good-byes. I never had the opportunity for closure. I would always feel grief from losing my daughter but maybe if I got to hug her one last time, I could heal more than I had. The following week I was given that opportunity. Stephanie did return through Silvia and I was able to hug her. We cried and held each other one last time. After Stephanie left, Laura came through and said that Silvia's grandmother had made a special agreement with Stephanie to be able to physically come through Silvia.

The following week, Stephanie came through again, this time in the cabinet and with Sid present. She validated what Laura had told us the previous week. When Silvia channeled Stephanie, she mimicked her exact personality and mannerism. I could feel the energy of my child there.

Sid maintained that it was important that physical manifestations be validated and experienced by all present in order to be considered real.

Sid said, "Stephanie gives us some validation that would be something that the medium does not know. Who is there with you?"

At first her answer was very vague. She said, "I have family here like my grandmother. And I have friends."

Sid urged her, "Stephanie, give us a name of someone there so we can validate."

She answered, "George."

George is my brother who died from lung cancer in 2006. He was twenty-four years my senior.

Sid asked her, "Stephanie, tell us something about George, something that he does that the medium would not know."

She responded, "Well, he smokes a pipe and it smells good."

I practically fell off of my chair. At some point in my brother's life, he did smoke a pipe, but I vaguely remembered it. I did remembered how everyone in the family commented that the pipe tobacco smelled good compared to cigarettes. He smoked the cherry flavored pipe tobacco. I later called my sister-in-law to validate. I asked her about the pipe-smoking incident and she said that it was when they lived in California in 1965. Without a doubt, this was Stephanie who had communicated with us.

Despite the communication I shared with my daughter, I still struggled with grief. I was extremely grateful for what I was able to experience with her, but nothing replaces having the physical presence of a loved one. Every night I had reoccurring nightmares. I shared the dream with Sid after suffering from it for over a year.

In the dream, I am not aware that she is gone but simply missing. I wander from place to place in search of her never able to find her. I told him that this would be my fear, my Hell, never finding my child again. No doubt this dream that haunted me was caused from my own fears. The mere fact that I told another person about it probably opened up something and made it possible for Stephanie to really come through. The first part was without a doubt a dream. I dreamt that Sid and I were preparing for a paranormal event when suddenly I got that feeling of panic and asked where she was. He pointed past me and said, "She's right behind you."

There she was sitting on the floor. He kept reassuring me that she was always with me, even when I couldn't see her.

On another night, something very odd happened. I wasn't quite sure if it was really a dream or if I was really awake and had a vision of her in my house. It was very real. I was awakened by a female entity that I had seen from time to time when receiving dream messages from loved ones. She is a tall, thin, beautiful guide. She never speaks but rather communicates telepathically with me. She has never told me her name. She led me to a different room in the house, the one that had been Stephanie's room. When the door opened, there she was,

Chapter Ten: Entranced

standing there looking at me. I grabbed her and hugged her tightly. I could physically feel her.

She said, "Mom, you've got to calm down. I don't want you to be sad. I want you to know that I'm always going to be with you, I can't ever leave you. I am always with you. I want you to know that this is really hard for me to come to you like this but I need you to calm down and not be so sad. Mom, I will never, ever leave you."

My guide and Stephanie disappeared. I found myself back in bed, awake. I went back to sleep, feeling comforted knowing that my daughter was still with me, no matter what. The following week, during our mediumship circle, Stephanie returned to Silvia in the cabinet.

I asked Stephanie about what she had been doing. I wanted her to discuss our conversation. Again, her answers were very vague. I asked her what happened the night before. She confirmed that we had talked the night before.

At first she said, "Well, I've been running through the house. I've been at the house a lot. I kept hoping you would notice but you never pay attention. You have to pay attention, Mom."

Then I asked her to tell me about last night. She said, "We talked."

I told her, "Yes, thank you. What did we talk about Steph?"

She said, "I told you I would always be with you, forever, mom, that I would never leave you."

But all of a sudden she broke down and began to sob and cry. She kept saying over and over again, "I don't want my mom to be sad."

This broke my heart to hear my daughter cry and not be able to do anything about it. I felt awful that I made her feel upset. I wanted to hold her but couldn't disturb the medium in the cabinet. She kept saying it, over and over again. I tried to comfort her.

Then Sid interrupted, "Stephanie," he said.

Like she always did during her life, she could turn the tears off as quickly as she had turned them on.

She immediately composed herself, "Yes, Mr. Sid."

Stephanie had fooled me like this many times during her life. I laughed with relief. I think this time she wanted me to realize how painful it was to see someone you love be inconsolable. I promised her that I would not let things get so out of control again. Sid moved her in another direction by getting her to discuss other concerns.

He asked her, "What happens to people when they commit suicide? Where do they go?"

She said, "That is very sad. Some spirits like us, like me, (but not me, I don't do it) they go and they heal them. People who commit suicide get healings from those spirits. The grandmother of this girl works there, she heals people. She calms them down and explains what will happen with them. They heal their hearts because they are very sad. Sometimes they have to go back to your world. They get to stay for a while in Heaven before they go back."

This was very interesting as she just validated reincarnation.

I asked her, "Where do bad people go?"

She continued, "Some go to sleep for a while. Sometimes they go to this place, it's like Time-Out, Mom. Then they get counseling."

I then asked, "But what about the really bad ones?"

"Well," She said, "the really bad ones get sent to another dimension."

Not only did she validate reincarnation but she also indicated that we all do not go to the same place. There is a lot of controversy about the existence of Hell. Even though it may be very different from what many of us imagine. There is definitely a separation between where those who lived a good life wind up as opposed to those who have hurt others.

Sid asked her to validate some of the loved ones for him or others in the room with us.

She said, "Your mother has been around all day. Do you want to tell her something?"

He told her, "I talk to mom all the time, she knows."

Stephanie laughed, "That's right, she's telling me that you've been talking to her all day."

Chapter Ten: Entranced

I then asked her if she remembered the day she left this world. Her answer surprised me.

She said, "Do you mean the time that I was there and I was your daughter? That time?"

Here again, she validated reincarnation. I answered, "Yes, that time. What did you experience? Did a family member come for you? Who did you see?"

She explained, "No family came for me. I guess you would call her my spirit guide, we call her *Nanny*. She came and said, 'Welcome Stephanie, you are back home,' and I followed her into the light. She knew me before, she is an angel. She was waiting for me. The light was like the sunshine coming up. Some spirits stay and don't go through the light. They look at their bodies but I didn't. They don't know what is going on. Some of them have to have family come and get them. I knew where I was going. This is home for me. I didn't feel any more pain and I knew it was time to go. This is where we come from. I am home now. I heard you cry but I had to go, Mom, I could not stay any longer."

This was only the beginning of what could be achieved in the séance room. Even though I would always grieve for my daughter, I felt that the experiences I had with her helped me heal much faster. I knew that my sadness was having a negative effect on her as well. I had to keep myself in check for her sake, just as I had always done during her life I had to be strong for her. Just as she had always made me so proud, I wanted her to be proud of me. Negative emotions cloud our ability to communicate with our loved ones. Those on that higher plane cannot reach us unless we are raising our vibration level.

I had promised her that I would not allow the negative emotions to get the best of me. I had to find ways to keep that promise.

Chapter Eleven
Back to the Table

The table tipping séance is a life changing experience. Each session is as unique as the individuals attending. It is a very personal and sacred experience, where one can make direct physical contact with a departed loved one, and know unequivocally that they are still present.

Sid discussed his first experience with the table:

At my first table tipping session in Casadega, one of the medium's guides had jumped into the table. What was really unique, that I had never heard happen before, was right before the table started moving we heard a loud knock on the wood on the center of the table. It was very loud. All of a sudden the table began to move. The guide moved the table around meeting everyone and giving everyone a hug. He paid particular attention to me and directing messages to me about my mediumship.

Then the table continued to move as we sang. The table came to me and I asked if it was my mother. The table began to jump up and down. My mother and I had a conversation through the table about my journey in Spiritualism. The table was spinning and rocking on the floor as if it was happy. No doubt it was truly my mother coming through applauding me for my journey.

It was the same session where my cousin felt for the first time a real presence. She had finally gotten a clear cut message from the other side. It helped her get a true understanding of metaphysics. My husband's grandfather had also come through during that session and we could smell his pipe tobacco.

The connection with the table is so incredibly healing. Even the most skeptical of people are often left speechless from their experience at the table.

About a year later, Magne, Daphne, and Sid visited the medium in Casadega again. This time they brought another friend, Rachel, with them. It was one of the most amazing sessions that I've ever experienced in a table tipping session. My mother once again came to the table and she kept pushing me back away from the table.

This particular medium had a cabinet in his table tipping room. This table kept hitting me and pushing me into the cabinet. Once inside, the presence of Spirit was so strong that it became very cold. As I would speak, you could see the fog exuding from my mouth.

It was extremely dark in the room and one could not really see too much but Rachel was directly next to the cabinet. The cabinet was made of three curtains. I could feel a small table pushing into the cabinet and bumping into me. At one point, the smaller table moved around the curtains and proceeded to jump into the cabinet up onto my lap. It jumped up and touched me on the cheek like a kiss then jumped down and back around behind the cabinet.

The medium had moved to the right side of the cabinet and his hand was on the table when the little table moved into the cabinet. Rachel witnessed that the small table had moved completely on its own. It was one of the most amazing experiences that I have ever had with a table. I believe that the spirit moving the table was most definitely my mother. It was the most memorable experience for me.

*****

Our channeling medium, Silvia, shared her first experience with table tipping with us. She came to the center to fine tune her already existing mediumship abilities having no idea the journey that would begin for her.

She explained:

Chapter Eleven: Back to the Table

Being a medium, I'm able to connect with most of my loved ones in one way or another but never my father. If he was sending messages, I was not aware of his signs. My father passed in a car accident 35 years ago when I was only 5 years old and since then, I have been trying to communicate with him without success until one night at the metaphysical center. We were doing a physical session of table tipping when he came through and let me know that he was still with me watching over me and very proud of the person that I am now. It is very hard to describe the love and blessing that I felt coming from him that night a love and approval that I have been waiting for more than 30 years, finally was validated for me on that "special night." Sid was able to describe things (the smell of burned cable from his accident, his uniform from when he played in a band and much more) from him that brought me back in the past when I was a little girl. Tears of joy and comfort came out without stopping. I will never forget this experience, where I finally got the feel that my father was still with me all the time. I really needed that validation of knowing that I still have a father that cares for me. For the rest of the night, I slept with my hand on my heart, feeling absolutely loved by him.

There are very few times in my life a spirit has come to me. My mediumship has been something I work at, to turn on and off effectively, or to see and hear more clearly. When I am doing mediumship work, I try to put myself into a trance state, to clear my mind, and to let go of my inhibitions and judgment. In this state, I am able to do good work. But there have been a few occasions in my life where, unprompted, a spirit has come to me, and in those moments I have seen them more clearly before me than I ever have in my trance state. The way they have appeared in these instances is sudden and unexpected, and it is as if they are standing right in front of me, and their words are as clear as day. The nature of these experiences is always jarring to me, because it is unlike any other spiritual experience I have had even out of all the mediumship work I have done in my life. I had one of these rare experiences at a table tipping séance. Since it was my first time in that environment, I wasn't trying to go into my trance state or to do mediumship work. I was simply there to observe how these mediums conducted their service and to see if I could learn something new. At one point, the table was said to be inhabited by the spirit of someone's partner who had died, and that this spirit often visited whenever they had a service. The sitter's conversation with the table had gone on for several minutes, and eventually the image of a woman appeared next to me. She was looking over to him, and said, "This is really sad." As she stood beside me, I looked over to him and the table sitting empty in front of him and I felt her sadness. She then said, "I wish he would let me go." She seemed distraught, as though his interactions with the table were preventing him from moving on and hindering her as well. Not knowing what to say, I told her I hope he does, too. This instance has stuck with me because it makes me wonder who or what, if anything, was in the table, if she was speaking to me.

As it turned out, this particular sitter was not completely honest with whom he wanted to communicate. It was later learned that the spirit was that of a former lover, not his wife as he had indicated. The man had never resolved the break up and had obsessed over her even more so after her passing. He fabricated that she was his wife when in fact, they had never married. His continued obsession with her, kept her from moving forward as she needed to by creating unfinished business for her.

The lesson for this situation was to always make sure that your sitters are being honest and have the best intent for what is best not only for themselves but for their loved one who has passed. We always assume that the sitter does have the loved one's best interest at heart. The best thing to do if it is revealed that someone is trying to tether a loved one to the earth plane is explain to that person that it's important to allow this person to ascend to their highest potential. Everything done when communicating with Spirit must be done with compassion for both the deceased and those left here who are grieving. One simple little prayer to help those on the other side is to light a

Chapter Eleven: Back to the Table

white candle for them and say, "I give you light, so you can give me light."

By releasing our intent to hold them to the physical, we not only help their spiritual journey but our relationship with them as well. Your relationships continue when your loved one has crossed over. It's just a different dynamic at that point. Unfortunately in this case, the young woman did not want him connecting to her in that way. Perhaps the room had not properly been cleared and consecrated before the session and someone more earthbound had come through. How to avoid this sort of thing will be addressed in a later chapter.

I recently encountered a widow who mentioned in a reading with me that she was contemplating getting her deceased loved one to reunite with her. At first I, of course, thought she was considering ending her own life. I began to counsel her, convincing her that it was important that she live out her life as God intended. She would reunite with her husband later.

"No," she explained, "that's not what I mean. I want him to return here to me."

Again, I misinterpreted her intent, this time assuming that she was talking about reincarnation. But again, she corrected me.

She said, "No, not that. There is another way."

She went on to tell me that she was hoping to have her loved one walk into another living person's body. I was horrified at the thought of how she might go about doing such a thing.

There is only so much we can control with our free will. Much of what is manifested in our lives comes from this. We cannot however, control and change God's will, karma, or others' free will. When someone attempts to manipulate God's will, it crosses all boundaries and laws of universe. In other words, it is simply not allowed!

Through various types of necromantic magic one can open a portal to the other side but only to that which is vibrating the closest to our physical world instead of those spirits who are in God's light. This is an extremely dangerous practice. Driven by grief, one can be tempted to attempt such an act but like Stephen King's *Pet Semetery*, the results will not be what they had intended. There are earthbound entities that would be interested in inhabiting another's body here on earth, but it probably would not be the person you knew. They may present themselves to you as that person but it is not them. People who have attempted such things risk opening themselves up to a walk in, a spirit that inhabits another's body. You cannot control another living person's will that way. Their spirits will not allow such an unholy alignment. Those who seek such an abomination are setting themselves up for serious spiritual repercussions. There are magical practitioners out there who promote such acts but best to steer clear of those especially if you are a medium. If you do encounter a client who suggests such a thing, I recommend advising them to discontinue any such practice. If they do not, it is best for you to discontinue connecting with Spirit for such a person. It is not safe for anyone concerned.

*****

Sometimes, not only do our loved ones pay us a visit but also our beloved pets that have also crossed over sometimes drop by to say hello. One of the most common questions people have about the afterlife is, "Do our pets continue in the afterlife and can they communicate with us?" The answer is yes. They do continue to live on the other side and they do reach out to comfort us.

One client and student of ours shared her first table tipping experience that brought forth a surprise for her:

I had been coming to the Metaphysical Resource Center for six months before I experienced my first table tipping session. I had avoided it because I was afraid it would freak me out. I was wrong. It ended up being the most beautiful and healing experience I've ever had.

My godfather had passed away well over a year before the session. Mediums had sensed him around me and given me messages from him. But not long before this session, maybe a few months before, one of his three cats I had adopted had to be

Chapter Eleven: Back to the Table

put to sleep. I was torn up by this decision, it was the first time that I had to handle such a thing, and the guilt was crushing me. To make it worse, only a few months before that, one of his other cats had died peacefully in my arms. The contrast of the two deaths of these loving animals made my grief even more severe and the guilt even harder to bear. The fact that the one cat was very sick and had lived well past the usual lifespan of a cat made no difference, I still felt like a murderer.

So it was on an April day that I decided to try the table tipping. I entered the room and was amazed when the table started moving. It didn't take long for my godfather to come through; my Paran, as I'd always called him. He and I had had a falling out about a year or so before his death, making my grief thicker. I asked him if he had forgiven me or if he was still upset with me. When I said this, the table began to hug me, gently rolling against my stomach. I started crying, feeling a sense of relief overwhelming me. Then I asked about the cats.

I was a little self-conscious. Other people there had asked after relatives, and here I was asking about cats. But my cats are family to me and these cats, in particular, had been a part of my godfather and a part of me. So I swallowed any pride and asked about them. Were they with him? Were they okay? Did I do the right thing with the cat that had to be put to sleep? Did she forgive me for having to do that? I was so distraught just thinking about her that I had trouble asking after her. That's when the table did something I can only describe as eerie yet amazing. The table lifted up and began to drag one of its feet across the floor. The table was making what appeared to be a groaning sound. It gave me chills. Sid Patrick said that it sounded as if my godfather was trying to speak to me. The tension continued to build within me as my mind raced through what he could be trying to say. Was he angry about what happened? Was he trying to tell me that I had done the wrong thing? The more the table groaned, the more frantic I felt about what it could possibly mean. We waited for what seemed like forever, but was probably a minute or less, as the table kept dragging its foot across the floor, groaning and groaning.

Finally, someone spoke up, "It sounds like a cat purring." The eerie groaning that was worrying me was actually the sound of a cat purring. The table repeated the sound a few times after that, clearly imitating the sound of a cat purring. It even had the weird raspy little rattle in the purr that the cat had when she was alive. I broke down in tears. I had my answer. She was okay. She didn't hate me for having her put to sleep. She was happy now.

I can't truly explain how I felt after the session. I was a different person. It was as if all the grief and regret and guilt that I had been storing were finally released. I felt lighter and freer than I had in months. I felt cleansed. It's a feeling that has led me to return to the table a few times since. While I enjoy each session at the table, none has compared to that first session for the simple fact that I can now say that my cat came through on the table.

*****

During one of our channeling sessions, Sid said that he saw Stephanie with a large black cat.

Stephanie called out, "That's my baby, Mr. Sid. He comes to visit me."

Sebastian was thirteen when we had lost him due to Feline AIDS. He was always her favorite and she called him "her baby." I asked Stephanie why did he only visit and did not live with her.

She replied, "Animals have their own place where they live. But they can come and visit. My baby visits me every day and rubs against me. He loves me."

One week later, during a table tipping session, Sid announced that he was seeing someone hold up a toy mouse and saying that is his name. Sid said, "The name is Mouse or Mousey."

"I have a cat named Mousey," I said.

Mousey was a fourteen-year-old ginger tabby that had grown up with Sebastian. He was now getting on in age and very

Chapter Eleven: Back to the Table

overweight. He stayed mostly indoors, but enjoyed the outdoors for a few hours a day, during nicer weather.

Sid went on, "I'm getting now, that he's a hunter, they are telling me."

I replied, "Well, my other cat is named Hunter but Stephanie named her after Sebastian, who was the alpha male not Mousey. Sebastian was the hunter."

Sid just shrugged his shoulders and moved on to the next thing that came forth for him. The following day, however, something very strange happened. I was sitting at my computer when suddenly I heard the sounds of two cats growling outside my window. I then caught a glimpse, out of the corner of my eye, of my fat Mousey lunging onto a neighborhood cat that had wandered into our yard. The two growled and howled as Mousey rolled with it across the yard, then chased it along the back fence then over the fence. I raced outside; terrified that Mousey would get hurt since he was never a fighter.

There he was crouched in the high grass along the back fence. His tail waived back and forth like a lion ready to attack its prey. He continued to make a low guttural growl much like Sebastian had done when he was protecting *his* territory. Eventually, he calmed down and I was able to coax him back inside. In fourteen years, he had never done something so bold. He was always the lazy cat, while Sebastian was the aggressive one. I cannot help but believe that Stephanie and Sebastian were showing what they could do. I think that Mousey channeled Sebastian. This was later confirmed during a channeling session with Silvia when Stephanie stepped forth.

She said, "My baby misses Mousey so much. And Mousey misses him. They spent so many years together like brothers, Mommy. My baby wanted to visit him! So he did."

Spirits of animals, like those of humans, can channel through other pets. Even in the animal world, love connects us beyond death.

Another client, a local psychologist, expressed her gratitude for her healing experience with table tipping:

Kalila Smith & Sid Patrick

As a Ph.D. in psychology and student of life, I have studied the metaphysical realm since the mid-1980s. I have attended séances before, but I had never been to a table tipping and was curious and excited to be invited one night to experience one. I found everyone who participated to be genuine, warm, and caring Spiritualists. I felt immediately at home with Kalila and Sid. They are brilliant, unassuming and down to earth people. In fact, I had an opportunity to get a reading with just about everyone at the table before the table tipping session began.

After the room was darkened and a prayer of protection was offered, we began to sing to raise the vibrational energy of the room. Our hands were on the table top, fingers spread and touching the fingers of the person next to us. We were running out of songs that we all knew, so I began to vocalize and everyone joined in. The table began to move and slid over to one of the participants who engaged with the spirit. In time, the table came my way and embraced me in a way that I knew it was my grandfather. He always hugged me quite tightly. I asked him questions and he responded. The table went to "visit" another participant but soon found its way back to me and I was visited this time by the father of my roommate. I experienced laughter, tears, and sheer joy and elation at being able to connect to people I cared about on the other side. It was a different experience from working with a medium or trance channeler and a very empowering evening for me. I got answers I needed for issues that were happening in my life.

One cannot dismiss what one cannot see clearly. I have studied and experienced the other side enough to know that the confirmations I have received have been spot on each time. I feel that I came away more knowledgeable, more comforted and more enlightened.

The key to everything in these sessions is validation. When Silvia channels Stephanie, I recognize her energy. Silvia did not know her. She could not possibly capture her essence like she does if not by channeling her. But in order to be recognized, everyone present must be able to agree that it was Stephanie.

Chapter Eleven: Back to the Table

The only way to do that is to have certain questions presented and answered in front of all who are present at a session. The séance room is a laboratory for Spirit. We push to the fullest potential in order to obtain validation from them.

This is very important when any spirit is channeling through a medium. There must be some kind of message from the spirit that the channeling medium could not possibly be aware of in order to consider it evidential. Since Stephanie had begun to speak through Silvia frequently, Sid worked her to get validation. He constantly quizzed her about various things in order to confirm that was in fact her spirit speaking. In this particular session concerning the cat, the medium had no way of knowing that during her life, Stephanie had referred to him as her baby. Silvia is highly allergic to cats. They are not a part of her world, therefore, not something that she would readily connect to. She would have no reason to bring up anything about a cat. She has never been to my home and knew nothing about whether I had pets.

Sid always explains what to expect when we begin any session. He reminds us all:

If you feel or see something, say it. We want you to say it. If we all see it, then it's real. It's not just your eyes playing tricks on you. We are all sharing the same vision. Table tipping is all about the connection and unity of everyone at the table. Whether you're new, whether you've been doing this for years, it's our hearts, our energy that connects during a séance and manifests material things. Anything is possible. I've seldom seen a séance that is the same as another, it's always something different.

Chapter Twelve
Sacred Journeys

During the first two years that followed my daughter's death, I received as many readings from different mediums that I could. Getting as much exposure to different mentors is important to any medium's development. I always enjoyed new visits from her. As a part of my spiritual journey, I also visited some sacred places. There are many places throughout the globe that are actually energy vortices that can rejuvenate our souls and awaken us to our true paths. Many of these locations were used as sacred sites to ancient civilizations.

My visit to the Mayan ruins in the Yucatan represented more than a curiosity for a possible past life connection. It was also a place of healing for me. While there, I visited a nearby beach where I could commune with the ocean and those spirits who resided within. By merely stepping into the water, I felt awakened and cleansed by the soothing ocean water. It is in the ocean that I can connect to ancient spirits in my lineage. The mother of the ocean, Yemaya, is one of the healers. She embraces all who seek her love and healing. The short time spent at the beach, represented a very special union with her spirit for me.

When I cannot get to an ocean, I partake in routine spiritual cleanses. Whenever we work with people on an energetic level, whether it is psychically or through mediumship, we pick up energy from their auras. When we work with people in general, we pick up energy that is not ours. Some of that energy can be toxic causing us to not be a clear channel for higher vibrational spirits. I constantly partake in sea salt and floral baths, Florida

Water splashes, and sage smudges of my home to keep it clear of energy that might not be conducive for higher spirits.

During my recent visit to study with medium masters in the United Kingdom (UK), I spent a long weekend with Sid in the Republic of Ireland for a little down time. Ireland is a very spiritual country. The ancient Druids were masters of healing and communicating with the other side. The area is rich in both Celtic and Norse traditions steeped into its hillsides. The early cultures told tales of otherworldly creatures such as giants, fairies, elves, unicorns, and leprechauns.

We took a spiritual tour of the area. High atop the hills, on the western border of county Meath just outside of Dublin, is Loughcrew. There we found an abundance of underground tombs dug deep into a hillside some dating back as far as five thousand years. Inside many of these tombs ancient symbols were carved into the stones. Much like the Mayan temples, many of the stones were arranged to follow the sunrise or sunset during the solstices and equinoxes. These sacred passageways were used as places of initiation and ceremony, where one could raise their vibrations.

Another sacred location on our journey was the Hill of Tara. It was the place of coronation of the high kings of early Irish civilization. Ancient tombs, stone configurations and a more modern cemetery are among the sites at Tara. It was here that St. Patrick visited the Druid king in the fifth century. Thus began the conversion of pagans into Christianity in Ireland. He made the first Celtic cross which represented the conversion, by taking the Latin cross and inserting the circle which represented the moon goddess. It symbolizes the union of opposites. It is a sign of rebirth and the ever continuing circle of life.

We also visited Monasterboice, an ancient Christian settlement founded in the late 5th century, by St. Buithe. Today nothing but a few ruins and a beautiful high Celtic cross remain as evidence of this sacred space. All along our journey in the Boyne Valley, we saw ancient ruins of monasteries that had long since been abandoned or destroyed by war. Just passing through these special places of worship was revitalizing to all of us. Just

Chapter Twelve: Sacred Journeys

being in a church or sacred space of any kind, or nature can clear negative energy and rejuvenate the soul which helps not only to keep us healthy but creates a better conduit to communicate with Spirit.

In order to truly open to Spirit, one must not only be clear of negative energy and emotions but must also be properly rested. One of the great killers of connection to Spirit is exhaustion. This applies to both physical and mental depletion. Over exertion of the body or the mind can lead to a poor ability to blend with Spirit. Also, having too much stress in one's life is another hazard. When the mind is cluttered with inner dialogue or stresses from work or personal drama, this inhibits the ability to be fully present with Spirit. Since connecting with Spirit happens in the right brain, one must be able to shut off the chatter of the left brain. Spirit comes across very subtly. The mind must be quiet in order to recognize when Spirit speaks. Getting proper rest is of the utmost importance.

After three days of soul searching in Ireland, we were ready to go to our destination in Wales where we studied under some of the most renowned mediums in the U.K. We flew on a small prop jet from Dublin to Cardiff then drove through the rugged Welsh countryside to the remote national forest of Brecon Beacons. Nestled in the hills was Buckland Hall, a grand country mansion. The sixty-two acre estate included botanical gardens as well as its own lake and heliport.

Our host was an international physical medium who brought together some of the top names in the world of mediums to work with us, taking our medium skills to another level. Regardless of which instructor was evaluating me, the message was always the same: the most important thing was sitting with Spirit. One instructor explained that she began sitting with Spirit one hour a day. Then she increased it to two hours a day. She began to want to sit with Spirit more and more.

This was the key to keeping in the power. Sitting with Spirit daily creates a special relationship. It opens the door for communication. It creates rapport with the other side. Without the commitment, there is no spiritual growth. This was the most important aspect of working with the other side. This is crucial in both mental and physical forms of mediumship.

One medium, a young man from Scotland, got so caught up in Spirit, he literally danced about trying to contain the energy within him. His words left his mouth faster than it could handle, he began to stutter during his messages. It was clear to see that he completely surrendered to Spirit, letting it take over. As he delivered a message from the brother of the mentor, who had been a physical medium, the lights flickered and dimmed several times during the message. The mentor medium was so elated she could barely contain herself. After he had delivered the message, she revealed to everyone that the dimming of the lights was an agreed sign that she and her brother discussed before his death. When the lights flickered, she would know it was him.

One of the more interesting workshops that I attended during the week was one by Medium & Spirit Artist Jan Dayton. I mentioned in chapter four my experience with painting the butterfly. Stephanie had communicated through several mediums that she wanted me to pursue art as well as music and singing. Needless to say, I pursued the first opportunity that was available to pursue that.

Art in any form is a right brain activity. It activates that part of the right brain that is responsible for psychic and mediumistic abilities. Through the arts, one can help develop one's sensitivity to psychic energy and connection to the spirit world.

We were grouped into pairs. The goal of the exercise was for each person to read the other. Instead of explaining what we were seeing or hearing to our sitter, we were to draw pictures. We would then explain our drawings to our sitter. My partner was a gentleman who lived in Wales near the manor house.

I sat quietly and opened myself up to Spirit. Before long, a man appeared in a fog. I felt that he was this person's father. Visions flashed in my mind's eye rapidly, as my hand drew what I was seeing.

I saw a large house that was rather rustic. I saw a living room area that contained a large wooden mantle over a fireplace and a red oriental pattern rug in front of it. On the rug sat a tri-colored

Chapter Twelve: Sacred Journeys

basset hound dog. I drew each detail then proceeded to explain my drawings to my sitter.

As I explained what I had seen to my sitter, he validated everything, except the dog. As it turned out, his father on the other side actually clued me into the fact that this man had been thinking about getting a new dog. He had been thinking about a basset hound. Every time I saw this dog in the vision, I saw his father appear giving a thumbs up indicating that he approved of the decision.

We then embarked on another artistic project to use as a psychic tool. During the break, I felt an urge to start drawing. Normally, I have very limited artistic ability. I can barely draw stick people. Within only a few short seconds, I had sketched out the head and neck of a unicorn. I knew for certain that Stephanie was with me. Not only can I not draw a horse's head much less a unicorn, the sketch that I made looked identical to her style of drawing. This was not my work. Now a skeptic might say that I pulled the image from my memory, but I would never be able to actually draw such an image. Without a doubt, Stephanie was using the paper and pencil to channel through me.

The next project was to make a Christmas decoration from a fir cone. There were small, round pieces of fabric and pillow stuffing. The idea was to take a bit of stuffing and put it inside the piece of fabric twisting the end shut. Then, with a knitting needle, we were to push the Christmas decoration into the cone. With each decoration inserted, we were instructed to meditate on a memory from a Christmas past. This was very easy for me because all I have are memories left in me. It was a bittersweet process. Tears welled up in my eyes as I sat there focusing on past Christmases when my children were small. Memories of my daughter flooded my entire being. When the cone was completely covered, we were instructed to infuse it with our emotions. A lot of emotions were put into this tiny decorative cone. We then read the cones for one another.

This is a very good way to develop one's connection to the psychic energy on someone else. With every touch, we infuse our life force into objects, animals, and other people. There is a constant exchange of energy going on at all time, with every encounter. When we intentionally put our emotions and life force into an object, that energy can be felt by someone else. In the case of a psychic or medium, a lot of information can be derived from such an object. This is how *psychometry* works. It is the ability to obtain information about a person from a personal belonging. By becoming in tune to the subtle energies of our memories, we can train ourselves to be more sensitive in reading the auric fields of those around us.

In the exercise we conducted, we purposely infused memories of our deceased loved ones into the object. This brought up information about those who had crossed over, enabling those of us acting as mediums to tune into those specific memories. Because the emotions are so strong in our memories, especially holiday memories of loved ones, the objects radiated the energy of those remembered vividly, creating a very strong connection.

When love connects us to another, it is a bond that cannot be severed even by death.

The Unicorn that was drawn during trance art class.

Chapter Thirteen
Mysteries Revealed

Receiving messages from the other side can be as simple as a loved one wanting to comfort someone left behind, or it can be a deep message. The medium develops a relationship with Spirit that is continually evolving. If the medium sets no limits on what he/she is willing to do with Spirit, then the connection is limitless.

We constantly try to obtain information about the other side during our sessions, especially, if Spirit is being channeled. We also push for advice on what we can do here, to make life better for everyone. During several channeling sessions, we were given a lot of valuable information in both areas.

Once the channeling medium becomes more comfortable with the process, it is easier for that person to enter a deeper state of trance. In the case of Silvia, that was when one of her ancestral spirits was able to connect giving messages to all. He was an indigenous tribal medicine man, a Shaman.

We could actually see when the overshadowing took place. The energy was seen as shiny orbs floating or vapors around the medium's head. Sometimes a shadow could be seen coming into the room then entering the cabinet. Usually in a seasoned medium, Spirit will speak immediately but in the case of the Shaman, he began his session with a series of vocalizations.

At first, like many who appeared for the first time, he did not remember his name but remembered what his job was within his tribe. He explained that he was one of the main guides for Silvia, one of several. He told us that different people have different numbers of spirits. He said that some people can have only one but others may have two or three. Then, there were others, like

Silvia, who had quite a few. He explained that he had been with her since she was born. He also explained that during his life he did not speak our language, but in Spirit, was able to do so.

He looked at Sid, "Do you have a question for me, sir?"

Sid answered, "Yes. We would like you to give us some of your wisdom. Is there a message for each one of us? It can be either about us or someone who has passed that we know. Please give each one of us a message."

The Shaman answered, "First, I want to thank you for giving me the opportunity to come back. I am very glad that you are doing this. Everyone needs words of wisdom. Sir, you are very busy. You have a very busy year coming ahead. You will be doing more work with this place. You will be very involved with it. You will come to a place where you will have to decide between this and your other job. You touch people. You heal them, just like I did. It is important work too, what you do. But you are very involved here. Your energy will increase pulling you here. My time here is different from your time on earth. But I can see that the word is getting out. People are learning."

He then turned to me. He sang a beautiful song.

He said, "Lady, the one with the long black hair, there is a song about the ladies in my language with their long black hair. My grandmother used to sing a lot. That song reminds me of you. Lady, you go too much. You must do one thing at a time. You need to stop the pace that you are going right now. Slow down. Your heart needs to stop the pace that it's going. You need to move on fast but then slow down. Take a rest. I want you to listen to your heart. Work at the same pace as your heart."

Then the Shaman turned to another medium that was in the room.

He said, "You have suffered a lot of loss. You have had a lot of pain. But you are strong. The tragedies are over. You have painful memories. You have learned what life is about and what is important about where you live on this planet earth. Give back a little to yourself too."

Sid asked him, "Spirit, give me a little word of confidence, just one word each."

Chapter Thirteen: Mysteries Revealed

The spirit responded, "Love is everything for you. Love moves you. That is your thing in life."

The Shaman then sang again. Then he told us goodbye. Silvia returned, remembering nothing of what had just happened.

*****

When conducting a séance or channeling session, it requires complete darkness or minimal lighting, using a red light so that we see any ectoplasm that might materialize. There has always been a great deal of controversy over whether physical phenomenon is best done in total darkness, or if some light should be acceptable. Some mediums insist on total darkness but this practice inhibits the sitters' abilities to observe what is going on in the physical séance. The point of any séance is to give comfort to the sitters by allowing them to experience physical phenomena from their loved one. When it comes to physical evidence, the best rule is that everyone must witness the phenomenon in order for it to be evidential. In order for this to occur, there must be some form of light present. A red light is often used because ectoplasm can be seen in red light but not in white light.

We attended a physical séance in which no light was allowed in the room. The windows were completely blackened out. A black, plastic sheath was placed over the door to keep light from leaking in from underneath. There were approximately forty sitters present, many of whom were also mediums. We were all checked for metal or for any type of cameras and/or recording devices before entering the room. We were required to remove all jewelry or tape it to our skin in the case of piercings because of the risk of it apporting. We were instructed where to sit by the medium according to the energy he was feeling. There was no moving air or ventilation in the room. It became very warm, very quickly. We were all instructed to hold hands.

The medium was seated inside the cabinet. Prior to entering the room, two sitters were selected to ensure that the medium was tied securely in the chair. The main reason to tie down the medium is to keep Spirit from thrashing him about due to involuntary muscle movements that can occur when Spirit overshadows a medium.

During his demonstration, we heard several voices coming from what was supposedly a voice box that had been formed from ectoplasm from the medium in the cabinet. One of the people who had come forth was a man who claimed to have completely manifested as a physical apparition. He answered questions. He walked around visiting several people in the room, touching them. Sid and I were each touched by this spirit. A different spirit also touched Sid, that of a small child.

We had also attended another similar séance but the attendants periodically allowed the light to be turned on to assure the sitters that the medium was still in his restraints in the cabinet. During that séance, I actually witnessed the medium being thrashed about, still connected to the chair. I saw him being thrown forward, almost falling out of the cabinet then violently yanked back inside. This type of thrashing about was consistent of what I had witnessed in other séances when Spirit overshadowed a medium. In that particular séance, even though there were times that we were only hearing voices in the dark, I saw ectoplasm forming high above us along the ceiling.

I have seen ectoplasm entering a medium's cabinet from above, surrounding the crown chakra area of the medium. I have also witnessed ectoplasm generated from the nose and mouth of mediums. It is believed that this organic matter is stored in the pancreas of mediums. Light can cause it to suck back into the medium causing injury.

With each session held in our séance room, Sid pushes Spirit further to open up to more possibilities. The goal ultimately is to have Spirit produce physical phenomena. One of the most important things to remember when working with Spirit is to never put limitations on Spirit. Spirit will take us as far as we can go. When we place limitations on them, they respect our boundaries. Spirit is limitless. When we are no longer confined to the physical body, we expand not only our knowledge, but our entire existence. Our perspective is completely different. Spirit

Chapter Thirteen: Mysteries Revealed

can be in several places at once. The only limitations are those we impose in our physical world.

In one session, Sid decided to steer Stephanie in a new direction, by getting her to discuss world events. He asked her, "So what do we do about what is going on in other parts of the world, the violence?"

She became very serious.

She said, "Well, that is very sad because they have a lot of hate inside of them for many generations. They keep passing the hate through from generation to generation. For so many years, like way before Jesus was born, people in those lands never got over the hate for each other. Their feelings are very low. Hate and anger are very low emotions. That is why they fight and kill each other. We need to send love to them. This country, where you live, brings people to them to touch them and tries to make them see things differently.

We live here with love and peace. We need to pray and send love. But it's still going to be a long way before you down there see some kind of change."

When Sid had her describe what happened to very bad people on the other side, her answers could not have possibly come from the medium. She referenced something from her life that only I could validate.

She said, "When we pass we come back home. We leave the negative energy down there. We don't remember it. It stays there on earth. We don't have negative energy here. Spirits who keep negative energy go somewhere else. They have to hang out there to decide if they want to be able to go to the light, just like time out. Remember Mom, when I was little and you would say, 'Stephanie, you have to be in time out now and think about what you did and whether you are sorry.' God gives them a chance to decide if they are sorry."

Sometimes they do, but sometimes they do not want to get better.

Silvia had no knowledge of how I disciplined my child. She has no children of her own. "Time out" really would not even be on her radar.

Stephanie continued, "Some people are afraid when they come here. They don't know what is happening. Some people do not know what the light is for. They are confused. When angels come for them, they get scared. They don't know what to do. Some of them have to have family members come get them because they won't go to the light. They have to see someone they know and trust to go forward. Sometimes if they refuse to go to the light, they go to that time out place, Mom.

Sometimes the angels come visit us. We have different places here. Some spirits like to live by themselves. Some live with others. The angels come by and we talk. The angels are my friends.

When someone down where you live needs help, we get together with the angels to talk about what we can do to help them. They are beautiful, Mom, they look like us, like a person. Some people look like they did when they were on earth. Most like to keep their forms from when they were young but some don't.

Sometimes I see God. He comes to visit. But sometimes I get busy. It's just like there. People have jobs and get busy. But when He visits, He's beautiful. He has bright, gold light around Him. We can see Him whenever we want. You can see him, too. We are a part of Him. He is your heart. If you look in the mirror, you can see Him in you."

One of the participants in the séance, Ashley, asked Stephanie some questions.

She said, "Stephanie, this is Ashley. Do you remember me? We danced at Midsouth Con for the party with the glow sticks. Did I see an angel the other day? I saw that person with white hair. I thought it was an angel. Was it?"

Stephanie said, "He had big white wings. I can see the angel around you floating very gently with wings around you. He's protecting you. He wants you to be more aware of things around you. He wants you to stay safe. When you see them, you ask for protection. You have to ask. That's why they let you see to remind you to ask for help. They can't help you if you don't ask."

Chapter Thirteen: Mysteries Revealed

Stephanie gave a message to Beth, another friend from Memphis who knew Stephanie in her life.

She told Beth, "Your grandmother has been following you around. She wants you to know that she loves you. She also wants you to know that she has been opening doors. She opens doors in your life so that good things will come for you. She wants you to notice her. Ask her to help you on what would be the best decision. That is what she wants me to tell you. Her energy is with you all the time. She will guide you to make the best decisions. She is pushing you to go back to school. She wants you to acknowledge her being there to help you. She's been trying very hard to get your attention, to notice that she's around."

Beth validated by saying that she had felt her grandmother's presence recently. She had been on her mind a lot.

When we traveled for our paranormal cruise, I put Stephanie's signs to the test. She had constantly told me that she sent signs but I did not pay attention. From start to finish on that trip, I paid attention. The goal was to see if Silvia would say anything related to what happened on the cruise if Stephanie came forth. During the cruise, I took a dance class. It was no coincidence that there was a Beyonce' *All the Single Ladies* dance class on the cruise I happened to be taking. I went, but was late. I could not get on stage. I sat in the audience and watched what was left of the short half-hour class.

Stephanie had also told me many times, through various mediums, that she wanted me to sing more. During one channeling session, I had promised her that I would sing on the cruise for her. Throughout the entire trip, my friends reminded me that I had promised to sing. They insisted I attend a karaoke session to fulfill my promise to my daughter. The song they chose for me was Harry Belafonte's *Banana Boat Song*. On one of the nights during the cruise, I waited for over an hour to sing the song for Stephanie. Oddly enough, as I waited, just about every song that was sung turned out to be songs that we used in the séance room. I felt certain that Stephanie was with me.

When I returned, Stephanie visited through Silvia the following day, just after a birthday party for one of my grandchildren. I coached Silvia into her trance state guiding her down the stairs to her special, safe place where she can communicate with her spirits. Silvia's breathing changed and she began to chant indicating that her great grandfather was coming through. After a series of chanting, bringing blessings, and protection to the room, we expected him to speak, but instead a tiny childlike voice came through, "Hi, Mom."

I answered, "Hi, my precious."

After she made the rounds greeting everyone in the circle, she told the group, "I am happy! I am happy about everything. The family was getting together. They were having so much fun."

Now Silvia had no idea that I had just left a family get together. But Stephanie knew.

She continued, "I was there, Mom. It was fun but you did not get me a hot dog again! I wanted a hot dog. I was looking for one. There was not one at that party. Next party, make sure you have hot dogs, Mommy."

Sid interrupted her, "So Steph; you came on the cruise with us because we saw you all over. What did you see us do? '

Stephanie said, "You were talking about us on the other side. Mom promised me that she would not be sad anymore. I am still waiting on you to paint, Mommy. I told you to do music. There was music for me. It made me happy. It was *All the Single Ladies*. Every time that song comes on, I am there. But Mom, you didn't dance. You were supposed to dance like I did, that's a good song. But you did sing. You made music for me. The song was in memory of me."

Sid then changed the tone of the conversation, steering her into the subject of reincarnation, again. Stephanie then became very serious again.

She said, "Some people want to go down there. But some who don't learn their lessons have to come back after they had time out. Some people just like to go back after they take a break. Some people just like the earth things. We go so we can grow as spirits for God.

Chapter Thirteen: Mysteries Revealed

The energy up here brought all of you together, so you all can help other people. You, Mr. Sid, and this medium are going to experience a lot, to grow. Everything you do down there on earth is to experience so you can grow for God.

Sometimes, Mom, you are too tired. Your energy is low. You have to take care of yourself. Remember when you used to put me in quiet time? We had quiet time so we could relax. You need quiet time, Mom. Quiet time, means no computers, no phones, just quiet. You need quiet so you can relax."

She also mentioned on several visits that some souls must be reborn immediately. This indicates that perhaps, if we fail to fulfill our soul's agreement to learn the lessons that this lifetime has for us, that we must return to repeat it. Many factors could alter this causing one to divert from what the original purpose was to learn in a particular incarnation.

Stephanie left me with words of wisdom. She gave me advice on what I needed to do for myself to help me better communicate with Spirit. She opened us up to what life is like in her new world. Death is not an ending. It is a crossing over into another world where we become more enlightened.

Chapter Fourteen
Hidden Dangers

A lot of people fear séances, mediumship, and communication boards. The biggest fear being that one will conjure a demon. Most demon hysteria is prompted by Hollywood. This idea is also promoted by over-zealous religious fanatics and some ghost enthusiasts. Many of these people have been fueled by the media which raises the fear factor with overly dramatic alleged demon activity. Very little of this has anything to do with reality. There are a lot of people who enjoy the adrenaline rush that these shows provide. I often encounter people who are addicted to this type of stimulation. They go out of their way to seek out frights. This *paranormal thrill-seeker* will push the envelope in getting others around them worked up, so naturally, things will manifest. This is not because of Spirit, but because of psychic energy caused by the fear and hysteria. This can create a cycle of terror that can create enough energy that one might believe that they have conjured a demon. In reality, these so-called demons are manifestations from the hysterical individual or group. Unfortunately, I had learned this lesson the hard way.

During one investigation that I had conducted for a television show, I was pressed for time so I collected information from the homeowner, who seemed to have done her homework. She originally contacted me claiming that a malevolent spirit of the former owner haunted her home. She informed me that a cult leader who conducted necromantic rituals previously owned the home. She told us that this man was an evil magician who conducted sexual orgies and animal sacrifices as part of his rituals. She said that he lured young men into his religion for sexual purposes. She went on to elaborate that the cult leader had died shortly before Katrina. Not too long thereafter, she had purchased the fully furnished house. One of her chief complaints was that all of the mirrors in the house had been painted over. She told us that she had replaced many of them with new mirrors that were now shattering with no physical cause. She also had found human remains under the subfloor of the house when she replaced the floor.

She appeared to be rational so I gave her the benefit of the doubt. There are certainly people out there, especially in New Orleans, who practice rituals based on the necromancy magic of Aleister Crowley. Crowley was a high ceremonial magician in the early 1900s who conducted rituals, which included trying to reanimate the dead. He created several magical orders that have followers to this day. What the homeowner had described sounded very much like something that might be related.

The investigation indicated that there was a male spirit who was present in the house. It felt as if he had been there for quite a long time. He did not seem to be malevolent but even the best psychics can be swayed when fed incorrect information. Once this information is provided, it is easy for the mind to create a story about a location. Even if the psychic is unaware of the initial history, if he/she is brought into a situation where people nearby are projecting their thoughts, that misinformation can be picked up distorting a situation. The only other thing I felt in the house was the presence of a female entity who seemed to be a former caretaker. She remained primarily on the second floor.

We conducted the investigation and filmed the episode. We encouraged the owner to have a cleansing done on the house to remove any residual energy. Shortly thereafter, another network wanted a property that included animals in the haunting. It just so happened that this particular woman had four dogs. I recommended the property to the network.

In just one short month after my visit, when I returned with the new network, the woman reported increased activity. More mirrors had broken. The dogs were even more agitated than

Chapter Fourteen: Hidden Dangers

before. It was as if whatever was in that house was kicked up over the increase in investigations…or so it seemed.

During the filming, the show's resident ghost hunters decided to attempt communication with the spirit. They used what is called a ghost box, which basically equates to a hacked AM radio that jumps channels non-stop. I am not a fan of these gadgets. I feel they leave a lot of margin for error making them a poor choice in validated spirit communication. I was invited to attend this session. I watched in horror as the celebrity ghost hunters baited this woman pushing her further into hysteria. The more hysterical she became, the more the ghostly activity increased. The more she reacted, the more they baited her. Finally, I realized what was going on.

This woman lived in the house with her very large family. The more she became unnerved, so did the other members of the house, including the four dogs. All of the psychic energy that was being thrown around by those in the home was creating what many might call poltergeist activity, which is actually psychic energy from the living. Things were falling off of the walls, mirrors breaking, and glass shattering which in turn, escalated the hysteria until it had become a vicious cycle. I also believe that she had begun to enjoy the attention of a couple television shows.

Towards the end of filming the second show, I ran into someone I know very well who asked about my goings on. I mentioned the property location to this person. Much to my surprise, this person knew the former owner. She confirmed that the man was a priest of a legitimate religion. Not only was he nothing like the new owner had portrayed him; he wasn't even dead. The man was elderly. He had become quite ill. He had spent the past several years in a nursing home, in a coma. None of the information provided by this new home owner was true. It was an invaluable lesson. This experience showed me how hysteria can create poltergeist type activity. This experience changed my perception of evil presences. It's easy to become convinced that something demonic is happening, when in fact, it is nothing more than an illusion.

This sort of hysteria happens all of the time. Recently, I had become overloaded with work, classes, workshops, circles, and family obligations. I was getting by on three to four hours sleep a night. I was working out but skipping my stretches and my yoga classes. My work days lasted twelve to fourteen hours. This went on seven days a week for an entire month.

By the end of the month, I was exhausted. I had spent months recuperating from an injury obtained in a motor vehicle accident. I prided myself always with not needing medications such as pain relievers or muscles relaxers, relying on natural remedies to rehabilitate myself. After nine months, I had finally gotten to a point where the pain in my left hip and lower back were minimal.

One late night after a very intense weekend, I took my dogs out for a walk. I was completely overworked. I had just finished packing my suitcase for an upcoming cruise. I had moments before taken off my favorite sandals, packing them into my bag. There was a pair of rubber flip-flops on the floor of the office. I stepped into them.

My first thought was, "Every time I wear these things, I practically kill myself. I really need to throw them away."

I dismissed any concerns about the flimsy shoes because I was only stepping out onto the patio in the backyard. I brought the dogs out as usual. As I walked across the patio, I felt a large bug on my arm. I jerked fast attempting to brush it off of my arm. I lost my balance falling directly onto the concrete flooring. I immediately reinjured myself, throwing the muscles into spasm, which created extreme pain.

Just prior to this mishap, I had been communicating with an individual who had an alleged cursed object that he wanted me to possibly film for him. I had agreed only to meet with him without the object. My intention was to coach him only on the process. I had no direct contact at that time with him or the object. He had shared many stories online about how people who encountered the object suffered injuries. I was scheduled to have a telephone conference with him the following day. When I contacted him to inform him that I needed to reschedule due to

Chapter Fourteen: Hidden Dangers

my fall, he suggested that the object was to blame for the accident. I was very tired and in a great deal of pain. The power of suggestion took over. Before long, he had me believing that the object played some role in the accident. He managed to convince me that spiritual energy was to blame.

Due to my experience with the television show I knew that our minds can create a lot of what we perceive as evil presences. I began to wonder if these items were really cursed or if the energy on them was manifested through the fear connected with them.

The next day, I visited a doctor. I was treated for my injury. After a good dose of anti-inflammatory medication that evening, I fell into a deep sleep. When I awoke the following morning, I felt my muscles relaxing much more than they had in months. I realized that all of my tension, along with not stretching adequately during my workout sessions, was to blame for my pain. I had taken many a fall before with the flimsy flip flops. Had my muscles not been so tense, the minor fall would have proven uneventful. There was nothing supernatural going on. There were no dark forces at work here, only my own neglect.

This is not to say that negative energies cannot be harmful or that demonic forces do not exist. They do. Some spiritual beings are higher vibrational beings, close to God's consciousness. They were never human. These energies go by many different names in various religions. Most of us are familiar with Angels. They usually work on our behalf aiding us in our spiritual path. They bring us closer to a higher consciousness. But not all spirits are ghosts or highly evolved entities like Angels. There are darker spirits that are detached from God's conscientiousness, those are what we know as demons.

These darker forces do not work on our behalf. High ceremonial magicians often call upon them for their specific purposes. That call usually requires a price to pay in return for services rendered. Although it is rare, it is quite possible that one can encounter these energies while working with hauntings. This is why many religions take issues with communication boards. The boards themselves are not evil, but unless you are trained in opening and closing portals to the other side, you should avoid such methods of communication. Earthbound entities can easily be contacted through these tools. They can cause chaos by misrepresenting their intentions to unsuspecting participants. It is only in very rare instances that one might stumble upon an actual demon. Should it be suspected that such a negative entity is present, it is important to contact the proper clergy who is trained in dealing with this sort of energy. Don't be conned by those who make claims to be "demonologists" but have no credentials. Playing with negative entities can be dangerous. It should never be taken lightly or dealt with anyone not trained to do so. If a person claims to be an expert in this field, ask for credentials. There are people who make such claims purely to satisfy their ego. Dabbling in dark arts usually serves only to make the situation worse. They can also cause enough residual chaotic energy to con you into believing there really is a demon present when there might actually be no intelligent entity at all.

Intent is the main thing when working with the spirit world. If you look for dark, spooky things, you will encounter them. There are specific laws in the universe that apply to all, regardless of belief systems or religion. One is the *law of attraction*. Whatever you focus your intent upon is what you either create or attract. If you are looking for trouble, you will find it. You will not attract negative entities by reading about them, watching a horror movie, taking a ghost tour, or listening to ghost stories. You can attract them if you dabble in black magic or necromantic rituals (cemetery rituals), hang out in cemeteries with the intent of finding entities, take something from a grave, or act disrespectful in sacred burial places. Many ghost hunters enjoy taking pictures in cemeteries at night because they can get a lot of phenomena on their photographs. Your loved ones are not hanging out in the graveyards. Earthbound negative discarnate spirits and guardians of burial grounds are. Neither of these should be taunted or challenged. Any time you work with any type of spirit, it should always be with the utmost respect. Ghost hunters as well as psychic/mediums should always perform regular spiritual cleanses along with house cleanses to rid

Chapter Fourteen: Hidden Dangers

themselves of residual energy from haunted locations. Psychics, mediums, and counselors should also cleanse to release emotional energy from other people. Good methods to clear negative energy is to burn sage, sprinkle salt water, holy water, or Florida water, use crystals to absorb the energy (always cleanse the crystals periodically), take salt baths, burn Frankincense or Sandalwood incense, to name a few. If you are ever in a situation where you feel uneasy, the easiest thing to do is to sing. Singing raises the vibration level which prevents lower energies from affecting you.

During a very stressful period of time this past spring, I learned the lesson of singing to bring myself back up. A family member had been quite ill for weeks. I was not only working but making frequent trips to the hospital. One evening, I was so over inundated with taking care of business and other people that I completely forgot that my jeep had very little gas in it.

On the commute home from work, I ran out of gas right on an exit in the middle of four cemeteries. I was very frazzled by the time I made it home. During the evening, I did manage to have one dream, one where a friend of mine appeared sitting on my bed. He had been a professional singer his entire life.

He showed up with a big smile on his face.

He said, "Everything is okay, Kat."

I responded, "It might be okay where you are but I'm in Hell. Nothing is going right."

"Just remember, when you feel down, sing," he told me.

He then began to sing songs that we sang during our sessions. Before long, he had me singing and laughing until I eventually woke feeling much better than the night before. I wrote if off as a silly dream.

The following day, Sid and I had a lunch meeting. I told him of my stressful evening. He said, "All you had to do was sing."

"Are you kidding me?" I laughed.

I told him about my dream the night before. He, of course, had already validated it for me. A couple of hours later, I was in session with another medium as we practiced. She gave me the same message. From that point forward, every time I had a reading from anyone, I was instructed to sing.

Another excellent method to ground yourself and discharge negative energy is to stand barefoot on the ground. Visualize the negative energy leaving your body, dissolving into the earth. Always finish up any type of spiritual session by envisioning yourself enveloped in the white light and the love of God.

The most important thing to remember is that most of everything in the universe is contingent upon intent. We should always approach any dealings with Spirit with respect and love. Unfortunately, even the most cautious Spiritualist can accidently encounter a negative entity, if the conditions are right for such a manifestation.

*****

Sid and a local Wiccan Priestess, Dr. Charlotte Pipes, were called to cleanse a home recommended by a medium from a popular television show after an investigation. The medium told the owner of the home to locate a local Wiccan Priestess to bless her home.

Upon arrival at the home Sid and Charlotte were met by the owner and her children. The family was taught how to create a psychic shield which is a form of metaphysical protection against negative energies.

The family stood in a circle a bit more than arms-length apart. They were to use creative visualization for this exercise. The family was then instructed to place their hands on their chest, close their eyes and visualize a tiny sparkle in their heart. Next, they were to imagine they were blowing up that tiny sparkle three times, as if they were blowing up a balloon. The first time, they would blow it up to the size of a regular basketball. Everyone inhaled and expanded their arms to the size of a basketball. On the next exhale, they blew the ball up to the size of a very large beach ball. On the third exhale they were instructed to blow it up past arms-length and now imagine they were inside this protective bubble of white light.

Chapter Fourteen: Hidden Dangers

The family was also instructed to use this technique whenever they felt frightened, excited, or scared. They were told that when they felt safe, they could deflate their shield by reversing the process. Inhaling and shrinking the shield down back to that shiny gold sparkle in their hearts.

Sid instructed the family on how energies do not have eyes, but rather they have polarities.

He said, "Therefore if you are feeling these energies pressing on your aura field, the quickest remedy is to shield, sing or pray, and walk away. Once you change your polarity they are unable to connect or feed from your energy. Remember, they need energy to stay on this physical plane."

During the cleansing phase of the home, they entered a room upstairs where the air felt heavy. The sage ignited with a flame. As it did, Charlotte turned to Sid.

She said "the sage knows".

She continued using her broom to whisk the smoke from the sage to all the rafters in the room. Sid followed anointing all windows, mirrors and door frames.

Suddenly, as the sage smoke was being whisked, the broom was pulled out of Charlotte's hand. It slammed to the floor. She retrieved it from the floor. She started again to whisk the smoke around the area. The broom was pulled out of her hand a second time. This time it flew across the room, slamming onto the floor. Charlotte grabbed it. She chanted her words of power as she whisked the broom again. The energy had become thicker. Both of them moving towards the door, Sid continued spraying the blessed water as Charlotte continued sweeping the sage smoke. When they reached the door, they pushed the energy ahead of them down the stairs.

There was a kitchen at the foot of the stairs with a table covered with the children's school books. As the energy was pushed down the stairs, the books slid across the table, knocking all of the books off. The owner of the home later acknowledged that the room was where the medium had felt the negative entity. The cleansing continued until the blessing was completed.

Chapter Fifteen
The Unwelcome Visitor

Part of a medium's job is to counsel their sitters as they process the experience of communication with a loved one. It can be a very emotional event for someone to receive a message from someone on the other side. Most sitters seek assistance from a medium in the hopes of receiving comfort about a loved one. But many, who have never sat with one before, are shocked when communication actually takes place. The sitter is sometimes not sure how to react in the moment. There is a great deal of emotional release during most sessions. Not only sadness but guilt, anger, and other negative emotions can remain in a room where the release occurs.

Anytime there is heavy emotional energy involved, there will be some of that residual energy left in a space. As noted in an earlier chapter, energy is constantly being exchanged between people and onto inanimate objects. When emotional discharges occur in a particular location, the energy remains there until it is cleared away through spiritual cleansing. Sometimes, even the most meticulous medium can wind up in a bad situation, due to residual negative energy. We all get busy and sometimes are not as careful as we should be. When our unexpected visitor came to call, we were caught up in a very busy season. It had been at least a week since the room had been cleansed. We had enjoyed a successful, but hectic, psychic fair the day before. There had been a lot of different people in and out all day. Psychic readings are often focused on solving problems for individuals on the physical plane. People seek out psychics for all sorts of life problems. Sometimes serious issues such as drug or alcohol abuse, abusive relationships, divorce, even depression or suicide are being contemplated. It is important to know where to draw the line and refer the individual to a professional for specific needs. Psychics are not counselors, unless also certified as such. They are not experienced to deal with substance abuse, abusive situations, or suicidal tendencies. These situations require more than a sage cleanse.

Several friends were visiting from Dallas that weekend. We began our table tipping session just as we had every other one.

Sid said, "We are going to begin the session holding hands. Once the prayers are said and we have opened the portal, we will place our hands on the table."

We started to sing. Usually as soon as the singing begins, the table proceeds to move. This night, the table was sluggish. After a couple of songs, Sid stopped to instruct the newcomers on what to expect.

He said, "If the table comes to you, you need to talk to it. If you do not talk, they will not continue to come through to you. If you bring in someone, for instance, your grandmother, do not ask for someone else. It takes a lot of energy for them to come through to communicate with you. We don't want them to stop and go look for someone else over there. You might have just lost your opportunity to talk to that person. So don't ask for any other spirit other than the one that you know is present. Also, when the table comes to you, take your time. Ask who it is and give the table time to respond. Once the table starts moving, it really moves. You'll know when it's someone for you because it will bump against you. You will know it's for you. When they come through, talk about memories. We have to keep the energy up so keep the conversation going. It takes a lot of energy to move the table.

If the table moves out of your reach, let it go. Don't try to follow it. It will come back, I promise."

We started to sing again. After several songs, even though the table had moved a bit, we still needed to raise the vibration. We all chanted *Ohm* in an attempt to raise the energy. We continued this for several minutes. We could tell that the table

Chapter Fifteen: The Unwelcome Visitor

was trying to move, so we continued. Finally the table moved but it was slow. The energy felt heavy that night.

I sensed a presence in the room. Sid could see the spirits about six inches above the table. For some reason, they were not connecting directly to the table.

"My hands hurt," I told the group.

The table vibrated but didn't move well. The group called out for Stephanie. Something was blocking her. Most of the people present were mediums so the issue was not with someone in attendance. After a while, we ran out of songs. Thinking perhaps that we were simply tired, we resorted to putting the CD on that we used during the mental séances. We sang along to the recorded songs. Several of us felt someone walking around and in between us as the room grew colder. The table finally moved although it seemed cumbersome. One by one different spirits came through and attempted to give messages to their loved ones.

Because some of the people were new to table tipping, there was a lot of hesitation and coaching from the more seasoned mediums. Even people who are accustomed to mental mediumship can become dumbfounded when a two hundred pound table begins to dance around and stand up on one leg. The experience is like nothing else. When a spirit is communicating like this, the moment is short lived. With each spirit, the table moved but remained very low to the floor.

It did not occur to us at first why this was happening. Sometimes, if one of the sitters at the table does not believe or there is fear, this can hinder Spirit's ability to work with physical phenomena. If one person sets limits to the experience, it will influence it for all who are involved. It was not until Stephanie came forward that it became apparent that something was very wrong with the session.

Normally she makes the table fly. But that night something was different.

"Stephanie, what's wrong? Don't you like the table?" I asked her.

The table moved slowly dragging against the floor. I sensed that her energy was different as well. She was not her usual bubbly self.

"Something's wrong here," I said.

We continued to attempt to communicate with her to see if we could determine what was different this time. She responded minimally. I began to feel very anxious. It frightened me to see her unable to bring forth her energy. At first we thought maybe she was trying to coax Sid into the cabinet. Sometimes, by putting the medium in the cabinet, the energy can be pulled up to assist in moving the table so it made sense at the time. The ectoplasm was thick, but it was higher up than usual, nearer the ceiling.

"We might achieve something totally different tonight," Sid said, "Maybe we'll get an apport. It is a full moon. We'll see."

Sid left the table moving to inside the cabinet. We resumed the music and sang along in an attempt to raise the energy. We stopped for a moment after seeing something flash in the corner of the room. We all sat quietly, waiting for what might happen next. The ectoplasm swirled above our heads.

After numerous failed attempts at raising the energy, I asked Sid, "Do you think maybe something more earthbound is here? That is what it is feeling like to me."

"No, I think maybe it's something else, maybe if we use more upbeat music," he responded.

He and I come from entirely different spiritual backgrounds. We have different perspectives of earthbound entities. He believed that as long as we protected ourselves when we opened the portal, everything was safe from lower vibrational entities. I disagreed. The next spirit that came through on the table proved to be something that was not of the light.

We felt the presence move the table. Several people shouted out, "Welcome, Spirit."

Sid asked, "Who are you here for, Spirit?"

There was no reply. I suggested that perhaps we all should introduce ourselves to the spirit. We went around the table, each one of us saying our names. Normally when we do this,

Chapter Fifteen: The Unwelcome Visitor

whichever spirit that is at the table will respond positively when their loved one speaks. This time there was no recognition from the particular one. As we continued, we became aware of some odd knocking sounds coming from the back corner of the room. The sounds seemed low to the floor rather than above. Sid rose from his chair. He attempted to walk around to the back of the room to investigate the sound, but soon realized that something, or someone, was blocking him.

I heard Sid say, "Okay."

He returned to his seat.

He leaned over and said to me, "I think we need to close the portal and leave the room."

"Why? What just happened?" I asked.

"We need to close the circle, I'll explain later," he said.

He proceeded to say the closing prayers and ended the session. Later, we discussed what he had experienced during the session. He told me that when he tried to move around the table, he ran into an entity.

"It was as solid as you or I," he told me, "I ran right into it. It told me to sit down."

He had seen several sitters earlier that weekend. Apparently, one of them had an earthbound spirit follow them into the room, who had decided to hang out for a while. Even though we had taken all precautions during our session to protect ourselves, this presence had already slipped in, undetected. The negative vibration connected with this entity prevented the higher vibrational spirits from fully connecting to the physical plane.

Although such a presence was not in any way demonic, it was still not the type of energy we wanted or needed in the séance room. We believe that the spirit became intrigued with the type of work we were doing in there. We do not know who the spirit was or what it wanted. It could very well have been someone who had passed recently, and for whatever reason, had not completely crossed over. Any negative emotion, such as fear, is enough to disrupt bringing in higher vibrational energy. This by no means indicates that the spirit itself was a bad person or evil spirit. It merely indicates that something was present that hindered the connection to the higher realm.

The lesson for us in that particular situation was that we always need to remember to clear and prepare the room before working on that level. It was a lesson we will not forget anytime soon.

We later learned that one of the psychics had conducted a cleansing of a client in the séance unbeknown to us. She had read a client who brought with them a family member who was engaged in substance abuse. These people had a lot of issues that should have been directed to a family counselor rather than this psychic taking it upon herself to resolve it by doing a cleanse of the people.

Sometimes psychics, mediums, spiritual initiates, are not adept enough to be conducting cleanses on the public. You must always go back to basic rule number one: energy cannot be destroyed. What many untrained people fail to realize is that when you remove negative energy, whether it be residual or an actual attached entity, it does not just disintegrate. It leaves one host and goes to another.

Another concern that often goes overlooked by those not formally trained to deal with clearings is whether the energy is indeed residual or is there an entity present that might be looking for a host. I have written repeatedly about the dangers of lower vibrational and earthbound entities. We all have free will on this level of existence. This continues on into the next dimension. This is why many Near Death Experiencers describe being aware of souls in the tunnel not moving towards the light.

There are countless reasons why a spirit would rather stay on the physical plane rather than moving on to be in God's presence. I believe in a loving, forgiving God who allows all to enter his kingdom. I see Hell as more as a disconnection from the Divine by refusing to feel worthy or refusing to accept the soul's responsibility for the choices made during its physical incarnation. I believe that there are some earthbound spirits who remain because they fear retribution. I also believe that there are those who remain because they are attached to addictions on the

Chapter Fifteen: The Unwelcome Visitor

physical plane. These types are the worst kind. They can become attached to the living or become walk-ins, an entity that enters the body of another living person.

These types of consuming spirits can possess another person, driving them to the same addictive behavior that they had during their lifetime. This is why it is a basic rule of any kind of working with the other side whether it is ghost hunting, or mediumship, those participating cannot drink alcohol or partake of recreational drug use. Places where this type of activity is common is where these entities reside. People who are partaking in this type of behavior often have these dark entities attached to them. Unless someone is qualified to remove such an attachment and knows what to do with it, it can transfer to another person. This kind of spirit serves only to use the physical body of another to access the addiction. This can be drugs, alcohol, sexual promiscuity, or even sadistic behavior and/or murder.

One of the most dangerous practices is the have someone who intentionally dabbles in dark magic such as necromancy step into a circle or séance with you. There are people who seek out not only earthbound spirits but other lower vibrational energies. There are countless grimoires (magical texts) that instruct the innocent on how to call forth spirits to "do their bidding."

Whenever this sort of activity is being practiced, it is very negative forces at hand. Nothing good can ever come of it. Never work with individuals who walk on a dark path. Usually, these people are very egotistical and will brag about their interactions with these entities. These people have a false sense of power. Their activity will include hanging out in cemeteries, invoking or evoking spirit beings to work on their behalf, or creating false relationships with entities whom they did not know in life, having no idea with whom or what they are communicating. This is why many people fear spirit communication. If the person is not raising their vibration, they could be pulling in something very low and negative. If any of this type of behavior is revealed in a reading, it is best to shut down the reading immediately.

Never try to cleanse or worse, exorcise, someone in a reading or séance room. If the person is seeking help, refer them to a qualified person who is trained in handling the situation.

Another type of situation to avoid is the psychic vampire. These can range from individuals who are benign but seek out endless interactions with psychics and/or mediums for constant attention to those who want what they believe is a power within you. These people can vary from those who are not aware that they have this trait to those who intentionally seek power.

I have seen many cases of what could be compared to a psychic form of Munchausen Syndrome. But rather than the individual pretending to be sick or physically injuring themselves for medical attention, the psychic variety will create supernatural drama for attention of a psychic or medium. These types thrive on "emergency" spiritual situations. These people continually need house cleanses because they believe that they are being plagued by negative entities, have spiritual threats, or attacks. Some of them are interacting with spirit beings that they believe are trying to coerce them into destructive behavior. Often times, the negative force is nothing more than a creation of their imagination given power by their fears or needs. Sometimes the person truly believes this fabrication to be true.

The other type of psychic vampire is what I call the Faux Practitioner. This is a person who claims to be more adept in psychic or mediumistic or even magical practices than they truly are. They want to be the mentor or the expert but fail to perform the work and dedication it takes to get to that level. These people seek out followers, whether it be students or sitters, then proceed to lead them down a false spiritual path. Either type is best avoided in spiritual situations because they bring to the circle or séance an energy which can prevent spiritual growth.

Even something as seemingly benign such as having a cocktail before going to séance can affect the outcome. Recently, some visitors came to a table tipping session after having a few innocent drinks with dinner. The energy that was left in the room when my circle came in to conduct trance affected our session. Even though we saged the room and burned some church

Chapter Fifteen: The Unwelcome Visitor

incense, it was not enough to clear what had been brought in by the visitors. When Silvia entered into trance instead of channeling one of her higher spirits, a young woman came through who was confused and afraid. When I asked what was the last thing she remembered, she painted a very dark picture of the last few minutes of her life.

She described running as someone chased her. She described a man chasing her through a wooded area. She then said she could see her body on the ground. She saw her jogging attire and the running shoes. She also saw blood coming from her head. This caused even more distress for her. She begged to go home to her husband. She said she did not know where she was. Apparently she was not yet aware that she had very recently died. She was somehow pulled into our séance room through the portal.

I asked her to look around for the light. When she found it, I told her to follow it. I told her that it would bring her home. I then told her to describe anyone around her. She finally said that she saw what appeared be an Angel. I told her to reach out to the Angel. As she described touching the Angel, Silvia's head thrashed back and a loud cry exuded from her as the young woman was pulled back from this physical plane into the light.

I immediately ended the session. When Silvia returned to the room, she felt drained and confused as to what had taken place. I later found out that these people had visited the room for a table tipping after having alcohol at some point during the evening. Even what might seem appropriate or innocent can easily take a wrong turn when working with the other side.

Lastly, never, ever bargain or give attention to a lower vibrational spirit. If it is a newly deceased person who is confused and needs directions, as in the case of what happened to Silvia, direct them to the Light or an Angel. Otherwise, it is best to let that spirit know that it is time to close the circle and that they must leave now.

Chapter Sixteen
Lifting the Veil

Halloween, 2014 proved to be a magical weekend for all of us. It had been a year since my first English séance with Sid. I woke up Halloween morning hearing several voices speaking to me. It was as though my room was filled with spirits. Each one was trying to get a message across to me. Whatever blocks I once had experienced were now gone. Visions flashed through my mind and voices spoke to me.

Halloween is the day that the veil between our physical world and the afterlife is the thinnest. Spirit communication is at its high point during this time. The veil begins to thin several days prior to Halloween then continues to remain open for a few days afterwards. For such a long time, my grief had blocked me from completely connecting on a higher level with Spirit. On this day, something had definitely changed.

The first spirit to make his presence known very strongly was a young man. When I see Spirit stepping forward, I see the entire person walking in from a fog. This particular man looked to be in his late twenties. He was dressed very casual but was clean cut. As soon as his details were established in my mind, the scene flashed to a sports car and some kind of accident. I became overwhelmed by a feeling that he had died quite suddenly, in a crash. I then heard him say that he had a message for his sister. In Spirit terms, this could mean a blood sister or someone who was as close as a sister.

He said, "Tell her that life is too short to spin your wheels in dead-end relationships or jobs. Cut your losses and move to situations that bring you joy. Find passion in your everyday life. You are wasting the best years of your life on people and things that do not bring you joy."

Just as he faded away, a little girl with blonde pigtails appeared from the fog. A stuffed teddy bear dangled from her hand. She smiled and faded away.

I began my busy day feeling certain that I would soon find out more about her brief visit. Throughout the morning, I found myself feeling elated, almost giddy. I realized that it was not my own feelings that I was experiencing. It was Stephanie's. Halloween was one of her favorite holidays. I could sense her presence in my house. Her energy was strong. Her essence vibrated not only all around me but through me. I could feel her happiness. I had blended with her spirit like nothing I had ever experienced before. I felt energized by her presence. I breezed through my workday and that evening's tour. By 9:30 PM, I found myself back at the metaphysical center, sitting in on one of Sid's galleries. I could not get the young man or the little girl out of my mind, but no situation arose that would have made it appropriate to speak out about them.

During the gallery, it was revealed that the young man did have a sister in the audience. He had unexpectedly passed. This seemed to have happened recently. His sister was grieving the loss very deeply. I gave her the message which she understood wholeheartedly. I could see the relief on her face of knowing that he was alright.

After the gallery, we began the mental séance. I put the memory of the two of them out of my head to focus on the séance. This year would be different because for the first time, Silvia would channel for the public. Thus far, she had been limited to channeling only in the séance room for those of us in the circle. The goal for her of course is to advance to give messages to anyone who needs it. Unbeknownst to her, my spirits had other plans for her that evening. Stephanie had been

Chapter Sixteen: Lifting the Veil

very active and obvious that day. The moment I got out of my car that evening, I felt Gary's presence as well. I could feel him pacing back and forth as if anxious to make his way through that night. It was Halloween, something that warranted the excitement.

We tied Silvia into her chair so she wouldn't flip out of the chair onto the floor, or move about the room in the dark. Upon Sid's instruction, I guided her into a deep trance state as music played in the background. I felt many loved ones enter the room. Immediately, Stephanie joined us. Silvia rocked back and forth in the large padded rocking chair.

"Stephanie is here," I announced.

"Hi, Stephanie!" everyone called out.

"Mommy, it's Halloween!" she exclaimed.

"Are you having fun?" I asked her.

"Yes! It's a beautiful night," she exclaimed.

"I felt you everywhere today," I told her.

"I'm always with you, Mommy," she told me.

"I know, but today especially, it's so much fun," I said.

"I know, I remember I used to get costumes and go trick or treat. Candy!" she shouted.

Then she became very solemn.

"Mr. Sid, you tied me up today," she told Sid.

"I had to tie the medium down, Stephanie," he responded.

Her mood immediately switched back to excitement.

"Mommy, mommy, thanks for the hot dog," she said.

"You are welcome. I'm glad you liked it," I answered.

As she chattered away, Sid and I became aware of a bright beam of light coming in from the front corner of the room. We could see sparkles of light coming in from the portal. We heard the wall on that side creak several times. Eventually, everyone in the room became aware of the activity there.

Stephanie announced, "Mommy, very soon a lot of babies are going to be reborn. They are going to reincarnate. They will be good people and they are coming to heal."

I took this an opportunity to question her more on the other side for our Halloween guests.

"Ok, so some souls are going to reincarnate now. So these are people who have been here before, is that correct?" I asked her.

"Yes. It is like a recycling," she told us.

The quiet in the room was broken by laughter of the participants.

Stephanie continued:

You have to understand. We go, then we come back home. Sometimes we stay here a long time. Sometimes we go right back quickly. Some like to go there and they keep going back. The ones who have a really hard time understanding bad things that they did take more time in another place so they can understand. Everybody has a chance to come back clean again and be sorry for doing bad things. They have to be sorry from their hearts. Some are sorry, some are not. The ones who are not go to that other place but they are the only ones who go there. They are isolated. They're very sad.

I asked her if she heard me when I asked her earlier to open the door for others' loved ones on that side to come through.

She answered, "They talk to them all the time. They just don't listen."

The silence in the room was broken by the laughter of everyone present. If nothing else, Stephanie was keeping them entertained. She was always coming up with a funny line her entire life.

Again, she became very solemn. She asked, "Hey Mr. Sid, can you let go of my hands? I want to give my Mommy a hug."

Chapter Sixteen: Lifting the Veil

The entire room was touched by her sweet request.

Then she followed it with, "I promise I'll be good. I don't want to be in time-out."

Once again, she had everyone in the room laughing.

Sid untied Silvia's hands from the chair and I got a huge hug from my daughter. Before the tears could leave my eyes, she instructed, "Don't cry, Mommy. It's Halloween!"

Sid asked if he could get a hug too so she hugged him.

He said to her, "I feel like I've known you all my life, Stephanie."

She responded, "You did, you just don't remember."

She then told me that she had several lifetimes. She said that some of them we shared. After we enjoyed singing to her favorite song, Stephanie left us and others came through. Sid noticed something move in behind Charlotte, who was seated across the circle from us. Unbeknownst to us, she, too, had gone into a deep trance. She later informed us that one of her own guides, a deceased friend and mentor, had visited her during our séance.

Charlotte explained:

In the days leading up to that night I had prayed to my deceased psychic friend, Debbora. I had invited her to join us at the séance. I specifically told her that there would be a medium to channel her; that she could speak to me individually or to the audience as a whole. I described to her the room we would be using, the details of the event and who would be participating. I assured her that everyone was open to the idea of hearing from her.

Once the séance began, I sat chuckling over Stephanie's antics. I felt a large, well-defined mass of energy come into the room. At first I thought it must be another spirit wanting to come through the medium to communicate with us. However, rather than move towards the medium, it honed it on me.

As it approached the mass seemed to get larger, denser, and more powerful. It was a very dynamic spirit being. It started pressing on my auric field. I could feel it condensing and thickening all around me. I closed my eyes and deployed a "psychic shield" – a protection technique. I felt the energy of the spirit being butt up against my psychic shield. Then suddenly, I realized what was happening. I whispered, "Debbora"?

Immediately the pressure stopped. I felt a huge void open up in the space all around me. I felt as if I had been transported from the séance room to another, much larger space. I felt as if I was suddenly suspended in a huge void. But it was no void. It was Debbora's massive aura.

I giggled and cried at the same time. I cried because I missed my friend, and giggled because death had not changed her one bit. She came to communicate with me directly that night.

As I prayed softly to her, thanking her, I felt suspended in space and only dimly aware of the rest of the room. I could still hear their voices, but they were muffled as if at a distance. At some point, I recall someone in the room checking on me to see if I was alright. I felt the vastness of her energy leave as I slowly returned to my awareness in the room.

What Debbora did that night was allow me to feel immortality. Through her energy, I felt what we really are. I was able to feel the amazing abilities our spirit forms have. We can be anywhere at any time by just thinking it. I felt that if I wanted to stand on the surface of Mars, I could be there in a moment. If I wanted to hover above the sun and watch a solar flare erupt, I could be there in an instant by just thinking it. That is the sensation of immortality. That marvelous state of existence is what we truly are. We are eternal spirits who have chosen to inhabit these fragile human bodies. I remember feeling the power of our true nature and thinking, "What possessed us to drop down into these confining, constraining bodies? These bodies that so limit our true abilities. Debbora showed me.

Chapter Sixteen: Lifting the Veil

During my trance, I saw a vision of the formation of our solar system. Our planet was just beginning to form out of the leftover gas and dust debris not already corralled and appropriated by our Sun. There was a separate energy signature. Amidst the dust and gas that was slowly starting to spin and eventually become our planet, there was a sentient being. That separate energy being became surrounded by the solar debris, and actually became incorporated into the new energy signature, that was our planet.

In the vision, I saw many light beings, Angels, watching our planet. Whatever is here with us is fascinating to the light beings in our region of space. We truly are light beings who have chosen to incarnate here and personally experience this fascinating planet.

Silvia's great grandfather, the Shaman, visited us again. He also spoke about the children who would soon come to our world. He spoke to all of us about being loving and kind to others. He spoke of people in our time who are too selfish. He said that people are too concerned with material things and what others can do for them. He instructed us to become more giving to others.

"People need to reach out to each other. Families need to sit and talk to one another," he told us.

He continued:

Families need to be more loving and caring for each other. We had wars, too. We used to fight, but now with the knowledge that humankind has, there is no need to fight. There is too much fighting and killing. Soon, there will be a new group being reborn. These will be people with good hearts. There are too many negative people down here. People should tell each other 'I love you. I care for you.'

As he spoke, I smelled sweet flowers and something cooking. I got a vision of women cooking something over a fire on a beach lined with palm trees and jungle. I could see the women making some sort of paste and placing inside banana leaves and laying them over the open fire. I announced what I was seeing.

Her great grandfather laughed. He told me:

We cook fish like that. We cook corn like that, too. They still do that. The women cook corn with milk and they wrap it in corn leaves or banana leaves. The women all get together and talk and cook. This is what life is supposed to be. They gather, cook, and eat together. They cherish each other.

Look into the eyes of your loved ones. Raise the vibration of the earth. This is why all of these new babies are going to be reborn to help heal the earth.

When her ancestor departed, then Gary came through. Coincidently, a friend of his was attending that night. The two had a chance to reconnect and reminisce about their past. Gary told us that he had forgotten a lot about his life. He explained that when he first crossed over, the healing spirits worked on him and took away a lot of his earth memories. He remembered the people in his life but some details of his life had been erased.

He told us:

When I moved here to this place, home, I first had to go to this place to kind of really forget a lot of things. There are spirits here who cleared a lot of memories from my mind that had happened in my life down there. Whatever difficulties one has down there, it's healed here. We are left only with the lessons for the soul.

After a brief visit, Gary left us and I brought Silvia back to the room. As I did that, the bar across the street music blared

Chapter Sixteen: Lifting the Veil

from the juke box. Bob Seger's *Down on Main Street* played and just as it did, the wall creaked in the corner where the portal had been.

Before his death, Gary was playing several gigs as a one man show. He performed a lot of cover songs and this particular one was one of them. He sang it every night that he performed at one of his regular gigs. The bar across the street had been quiet the entire evening so for that song to suddenly blast out of the place immediately upon his leaving and walls creaking, we all knew it was no coincidence. It was his way of validating his visit.

We continued to conduct galleries and private sessions the remainder of the weekend. The lifting of the veil really brought the spirits forward. They were all very excited to be able to visit. We topped off the Halloween weekend with a dumb supper on Sunday afternoon. People came and ate in silence with their loved ones who had passed. It was a very moving experience. Some cried bittersweet tears, as they felt the presence of their spirits. The little girl with the blonde hair returned. She hid behind my ancestor altar, poking her head out at me like a game of hide and go seek. I finally realized that she was my own child, my little Jennifer. She wanted to show herself to me. Her sister's excitement over Halloween made her curious. During sessions with Silvia channeling Stephanie, I learned that she often told Jennifer stories about "Mommy" and shared what her life was like. Jennifer had no regrets about her decision to not incarnate but she did want to give me the gift to see what she might have been like as a child here on earth.

Stephanie's message spun through my head over and over again that weekend. How would I know that these children she spoke of would actually be born?

Two weeks later a friend sent me a link to a local newscast. It showed a photograph of a hospital nursery full of newborn babies. It was titled *Baby Boom Occurs Nine Months After Arctic Blast*.

Chapter Seventeen
Science Validates Spirit

The key to all mediumship is validation. The holy grail of mediumship is physical validation that everyone present witnesses. I was fortunate enough to have this happen not once but twice and both times in Memphis. The first time was in November 2015, while attending the Memphis Comic and Fantasy Convention. Despite that fact that they focus mainly on fantasy and comic material, the con does have a paranormal track as well. That track is managed by Stephen Guenther and Tanya Vandesteeg of the Mid-South Paranormal Society. They also operate haunted tours in downtown Memphis through The Broom Closet owned by Stephen and his fiancée, Emily Fulghum.

I have worked with Stephen and Tanya on numerous investigations over the years. They had frequently invited me to be a guest at the con. This time, Stephen had also invited me to offer a mediumship demonstration in the basement of the shop after the tour was conducted.

Tanya, Stephen, and Emily attended a gallery with me and Sid during a paranormal cruise prior to this visit. The rest of the participants were customers who had never attended a gallery style demonstration of mediumship.

I like to take a few moments before I connect with Spirit. For me, taking the time to get out of the left part of my brain, and really doing a shift is important to me. As mentioned in previous chapters, it is of the utmost importance for mediums to raise their vibration by sitting in the power in order to reach the higher vibrational spirits. This makes the difference between just talking to earthbound entities and really connecting to the higher realms.

I spent several minutes in Emily's reading room preparing myself for the evening. Immediately, I became aware of a portal towards the right back corner of the space. A large mirror strategically placed at the portal amplified that energy directing it back into the room. I could feel a pulsing sensation emanating from the room. While Tanya conducted a short tour of the area, I sat in silence focusing on raising my energy. By the time she returned with those who were to receive readings, loved ones of those who were going to attend were lined up at the portal like race horses at the gate. When I stepped out onto the platform to perform the demonstration, Stephen surprised me with a little something extra. Along with about a dozen sitters was not only Stephen, Tanya, and Emily but the entire Mid-South Paranormal Team, complete with EMF meters. Stephen placed a table version on a small table in the front of the semi-circle of chairs along with a tambourine hanging from the ceiling. Across the back of the room sat the team of paranormal investigators poised and ready to make note of any changes in energy levels. Before he explained, I could already see where this was going.

"I hope you don't mind if we take some notes on what kind of activity we get while you are reading the audience," he said.

Of course, I said that I was fine with it. After all, despite the fact that I was very intimidated by the fear that they might get nothing, once everything was in place, there was no turning back. I took a deep breath and began tuning into those who were waiting to give their loved ones messages.

Once I got into the power, I paid little attention to the team and their reactions to my readings. I opened completely to Spirit allowing all those who were ready to step forward with their messages. During the demonstration, I couldn't help but notice that the tambourine was swinging wildly in rhythm with my messages. The table top meter was also lighting up in response to my connection to Spirit. At the end of the reading, the team commented on how each of their meters was hitting high energy levels the entire session. Once I announced that Spirit had left the room, the meters immediately dropped back to normal. I was elated at the results. In addition to offering recognizable validation to everyone present, I had physical proof of Spirit's presence in the room.

I returned to Memphis the following March for Mid-South Con. On this visit, in addition to offering another gallery, I conducted a Level I Mediumship Class at the Broom Closet. We conducted the evening exactly as we did in November. When Tanya began her tour of downtown Memphis, I went downstairs into the reading room to meditate. This time, I noticed that two new table meters had been put out on the table along with the usual hanging tambourine. I had high expectations of physical phenomena that evening.

The energy was already high when I entered the room. I rearranged the mirror a bit to help open the portal. Within seconds of going into meditation, I saw them arrive. Each one of them was excited to have the opportunity to communicate with their loved ones. One of the first to greet me was Emily's mother. Her presence was always strong in the store and around Emily. I let Emily know right away when I began the demonstration. This having been her third reading with me, she expected her mother to come through with a message for her. She shared her experience:

Each time that I have attended a gallery with Kalila my mother has come through to comfort me. While visiting New Orleans, she even came to me during a table tipping session. The last of these gallery readings, however, was the most poignant for me. My mother had been on my mind a lot. I had been worrying about her; afraid that she had not experienced the love and support from a partner the way that I do with Stephen. But during this reading, she came through to let me know that she had in fact found that kind of love with an old sweetheart who died years before she did. It did me a lot of good to know that.

I also participated in the mediumship class offered at the shop. My hopes were that the class would help me build my intuition and confidence with working on the spiritual realm. I did not, however, have any preconceived expectations. I was pleasantly surprised when I was able to give a validated message to another attendee at the end of the class. My experiences with mediumship have since led me to form a group here in Memphis. We now conduct circle a couple of times a month.

During our sessions, we use a KII meter and a REM pod just as we did during Kalila's demonstration. We also have a paranormal team who investigates haunted locations in the area. The store which is really haunted by a sordid history is the ending point of our downtown tour. Participants are allowed to conduct a mini investigation in the basement. Most nights, the meters sound off multiple times. We have seen the tambourine swinging without assistance as well.

Since starting the mediumship circles here, the paranormal activity has increased. There has been an increase in the amount of bumps and thumps heard throughout the building. During the tours, there have been a couple of instances where the benches upstairs had been moved without assistance.

Once, a group saw a large shadowy figure moving around downstairs. Another afternoon we had been playing with the REM pod downstairs and forgot to turn it off. After we had come back upstairs, it went off. It seems like during the tours, there are more meaningful connections made via the spirit box than before.

Physical phenomena manifests in various forms. It can be as simple as a tambourine suspended from the ceiling, moving back and forth or as elaborate as electromagnetic meters spiking. I conducted a reading for a sitter who had lost her partner recently.

Chapter Seventeen: Science Validates Spirit

After I read her, she pulled out her phone and played an audio file for me. It contained a form of physical evidence called *electronic voice phenomena* or EVP. When she played back the file, it clearly contained a whisper overlaying the original recording which said, "I'm doing this for you."

Physical evidence can also be experienced in the form of knocks on a wall. Sid often encourages sitters to attempt communication with their loved ones by asking them to knock on a wall. As time goes on, the sitter asks for two knocks, then three. It is a simple form of communication but is proven as an effective method of making contact with the other side.

As mentioned in earlier chapters, Spirit is limitless. Once you develop your language and symbols, the possibilities continue to expand as does your relationship with Spirit. Expect to be surprised even entertained by those endless possibilities. One of the things I noticed when I was being monitored by the meters is that they generally responded when I was not paying attention to them. This can be very entertaining to an audience of sitters when the medium and Spirit can play off of one another. For instance, during my first visit to Memphis, one sitter's grandmother seemed to enjoy making the meter light up while I delivered her message but only when my back was turned. When someone in the audience would laugh or encourage me to turn and look, she stopped. I was able to turn it into quite a little comedy routine between us which really added to the entertainment value of the demonstration. The energy in a room can sometimes sink making it more difficult to stay in the Power. This can occur when sitters are heavy in their grief. A little comic relief can pick up those low vibrations and Spirit knows this.

During my second visit, I encountered another situation that proved to be equally amusing to those present. I always like to see everyone in the audience get a message of some kind. In large groups, this is usually not possible but if the group is smaller and time allows, I like to ask those who did not receive a message to stand up. I give "something" to them so they do not walk away feeling like they attended for nothing. I brought my Tarot deck and asked those who did not get a message from a loved one to pull a card and allow me to give them a psychic message.

It is at this time, I explain again, as I had before the session began, that not everyone hears from their loved ones. I go on to explain that sometimes it is a message about themselves that they need to hear. As I went around the room giving out the psychic messages, I came upon a woman who was obviously hoping for a message from someone special to her. I felt bad because it was clear that although she tried to hide it, she was very disappointed with her experience of that evening.

I asked her, "Who were you hoping to hear from tonight?"

She responded, "My son."

This really hit home for me. I know how it feels to lose a child wanting nothing more than to hear from that child. A parent can never get too much validation that their child is still with them. I asked her to focus on him and I tried to pick up on him. Nothing happened. As I attempted to apologize to her and fumble through why he was not coming through, the entire audience laughed. I turned and saw that the meter was lighting up like a Christmas tree as if trying to get our attention. It then became apparent to me that her son was choosing not to come through me but rather attempting to communicate directly to her. I asked her if she heard from him in dreams. She very happily responded that she had. Then suddenly something else occurred to me. I asked her, "What kind of work did your son do when he was here?"

She answered, "He was a medium."

My suspicions were confirmed that he purposely was not coming through me. He wanted her to communicate directly with him not a third party. In this instance, science validated that

Chapter Seventeen: Science Validates Spirit

Spirit controls what a medium is allowed to see, hear, feel, and experience. We are merely the vessels through which they can choose to use to touch a loved one or not. This was an interesting lesson not only for the sitters that night but also for the medium.

Chapter Eighteen
Your Own Séance Experiments

After a couple of years studying the art of séance, many things had been made clear to our study group. We have shared our findings with others in order to help them create the space for their own séance experiments. Many new mediums want to know how to move into physical mediumship. There are specific steps that should be taken if this is the path you wish to take.

- A cohesive group is the best group that will collect the most evidence.
- The terms Spirit, Energy, Consciousness and Vibrations are all synonymous terms.
- A group that forms should also meet at the same time on a regular basis.
- In order to be phenomena, all in the group must witness the same thing at the same time.
- A séance should be conducted in the dark or infrared lighting until continued phenomena occurs.
- Allow one medium to develop that is chosen by the group.
- To be a sitter is a privilege, for it allows you to witness the phenomena.
- There are two forms of ectoplasm, energetic and physical.
- The best way to achieve phenomena is to be open to it.
- There are many ways to raise the vibration and is necessary to create phenomena.

All of these points must be taken into consideration as the first step in creating space for your own séance experiments. Before one can decide if physical mediumship is something they wish to commit to, they must first be introduced to mental mediumship. One should be reasonably adept with mental mediumship before taking things to the physical level. The first step is to find a mentor in your area. You should also be willing to travel to experience various methods with various mentors to assist in your development. You must have some concept of energy and metaphysical principles before you begin. Understanding the basics would be the first hurdle then onto a first level mental mediumship enfoldment class. It would be at this point that one would want to join others on the same level of development to form a mediumship circle in order to practice on one another.

When I taught the level one development class in Memphis, for the most part, those attendees were already familiar with one another through their religious circle. Because they were well familiar with energy and psychic phenomena, many had been psychic readers for years, it was easy for them to change gears and get into medium mode.

The class took place in the basement of the Broom Closet in downtown Memphis. This worked well for the group because they had already been conducting their religious ceremonies and rituals there and the space was well energized with a very high and positive vibration. As proven during my gallery sessions, it was very conducive to bringing in the higher spirits quite easily.

Because the group was so cohesive, they blended well together and everyone agreed to create an ongoing mental circle that would meet regularly. This group has excellent potential for moving into physical phenomena due to the energy in the room as well as the cohesiveness of the group. It is of course recommended that before physical mediumship, all participants at least complete an intermediate level of mediumship training.

Cohesiveness of a group is one of the most important steps in developing a séance group where phenomena occur. To study further, one must first grasp the basic principles as outlined in this chapter. Organizing a group to hold séances takes much dedication and understanding. All must be willing to commit to a journey of raising ones consciousness. All must agree that the

Chapter Eighteen: Your Own Séance Experiments

intent is to bring forth high vibrational spirits and not engage in the darker side of spirit communication. The best groups are those who are in each other's lives outside of the circle, as in the case with the Memphis group.

All members should place all personal feelings aside focusing only on raising the consciousness of the group. The energetic vibration of the group should always be first. There should never be an agenda or any form of drama within the group. If anyone is asked to leave the group, there should be no bad feelings. Keeping in mind this is to be treated like a research project with a common goal.

Everyone in the group should have learned about séance before starting. All things in life are made of energy. Therefore understanding how the terms Spirit, Energy, Consciousness and Vibrations are synonymous. Before creating a group, most should seek out and locate another group that has reached a state of producing phenomena on a continual basis. Once phenomena continue, others are usually invited to share the experience. This will give your group a chance to experience and determine how to start and focus their group.

When creating your group you are making a date with Spirit. This is why choosing a group that can meet on a regular basis at the same time is important. Spirit will understand illness and the occasional vacation but there needs to be plans for the latter. Not showing up or conducting is not respectful of the group or Spirit. Consistency is important if you want to see phenomena.

People will experience many things during a séance. Experience will include but not limited to, being touched, seeing shadows, seeing colored lights, visualizing an energetic grid, seeing ectoplasm being formed, moving objects, apportations and deportations, materializations, climate changes, trance states and more. The main fact is that every one of the sitters must see the same thing at the same time to be considered validated. Spirit is limitless.

Though there are known tribes in Africa that can produce the faces of Spirit in daylight, séances should always be started while sitting in the dark. Darkness is recommended until phenomena starts. After the phenomena starts, you can try advancing to infrared light. Usually Spirit will let you know when you can advance. Direct light in some cases can harm a medium by causing the ectoplasm to retract without changing its acidity, thus harming or even killing the medium.

Helen Duncan was a physical medium in the early twentieth century who died after ectoplasm reportedly retracted into her body after a door was opened as she produced ectoplasm in a trance state. Modern day physical mediums have also claimed to have suffered injury from ectoplasm under similar situations. This is why strict controls are important in séance when a medium is producing physical ectoplasm. Today it is appropriate for a medium who is working in a teaching environment to always work in an environment with the use red light. This is to allow a student to see how the phenomenon is created. Usually orbs or those tiny sparkles of light and ectoplasm will not be visible in white light anyway so stick with red.

Creating a group can be a challenge itself. One of the greatest challenges will be deciding who should be the medium. Do not let this cause conflict in the group. The person should be fairly elected by the group. This should be done by selecting someone who works the best with energy. Remember the purpose is to create phenomena. Get your egos out of the way. In my group, I usually play the conscious medium for the group, and Silvia is our trance medium. Most table tipping sessions require two mediums, one who is taking charge of the session and the other who is in trance.

Being a sitter is actually the most important part of the group and the luckiest. A medium rarely gets to see or experience the phenomena for they are usually in trance and/or stuck in cabinet. Spirit will work with each sitter learning their consciousness. Spirit will never let the group experience more than it can handle.

Spirit uses ectoplasm in different forms in different ways. In the movie, *The Scole Experiment,* Robin Foy and his group witnessed incredible phenomena with the use of energetic phenomena. In our studies, energetic ectoplasm was most prevalent as well. Physical ectoplasm is created by a medium.

Chapter Eighteen: Your Own Séance Experiments

This is a chemical substance produced by the body that leaves the medium's body via any orifice. In most cases, it looks almost like a cheese cloth substance. You can find many a picture on the internet. To learn more about energetic ectoplasm you can join Robin Foy's website, *physicalmediumship4u.ning.com*.

Raising the vibration is a key step in assisting Spirit to connect to our physical world. Singing, praying, and chanting are just some of the ways to increase the vibrations. Putting ionized air into the room will also assist in Spirit connection. Always remember to cleanse your séance room on a regular basis.

Also, opening and closing the portals at the beginning and end of each session is probably the most important task within the séance. Protecting everyone in the group in God's white light and love is essential as well. Séance forming is not a joke or should ever be used in fun for it can be dangerous.

In summation, research and study is highly recommended before developing a group. The book *Séance Experiments* is only to be used as a resource or for an understanding of a higher connection with Spirit. Before starting a group, if there are any questions, you can send them to our FaceBook page, *https://www.facebook.com/seanceexperiments*. You can also see here when we might be in your area conducting a Spirit study. Open your hearts and the world of Spirit is at your fingertips.

Chapter Nineteen
Adventures in the Cabinet
(Sid Patrick)

During my initial journey to Arthur Findley College in Stanstead, England, I was fortunate enough to be exposed to many miraculous interactions with Spirit. I was blessed with studying under the infamous Spiritual tutor, Glyn Edwards. Glyn was more than your average tutor. He was on the senior staff of AFC for more than thirty years. His journey began when he was sixteen when he joined the Benedictine community. His spiritual works have encouraged many on their journey into working with Spirit.

While studying with Glyn, I was encouraged to take a workshop with a young physical medium. His name was Scott. He was one of the many tutors that demonstrated at AFC during that time. While Glyn was phenomenal in trance, mental and physical mediumship, Scott was one of the best I have encountered in demonstration.

On the day that Glyn created an energy circle and after my moment of clarity (with the flowers on the bed mentioned in an earlier chapter), I soon became rather ill. I was supposed to attend a table tipping in the sanctuary room that evening. Instead, I opted for a nap. When I awoke in my room, I thought I needed to take a walk. There were two groups of séance demonstrations. I was already appointed to the second group that was scheduled for the following night. I knew there was one currently going on in the main hall so I ventured that way. Upon my arrival to the dimly lit hall, I could hear laughter and singing. Having never been exposed to a séance before, that was the last thing I expected to hear.

My idea of a séance at that time was the Hollywood stereotype; everyone sitting at a big table holding hands summoning the dead. There may have been a candle or two lit. There, a medium would begin to go in trance and then things would start to happen. This, of course, was just what I had learned from movies. But now, I was hearing people signing and laughing. I heard drums banging. The hall was filled with energy even though it was all taking place in a locked study. I could not wait for my turn in the séance room the following night. My imagination ran wild with anticipation for what might happen behind those doors.

The following day, we were invited to a pre-séance class in which we were instructed of the protocol for Scott's séance. We were told that we would be patted down then checked with a metal detector. We were also told what we were allowed to wear along with what not to wear. There were instructions on how our seat would be determined and how to react when Spirit spoke to us. Clapping, bathroom privileges, or moving about were not permitted. Hands were to be held the entire séance unless otherwise noted from Spirit. Scott then threw two pieces of crumpled paper in a ball into the group. Two of the people in one of my other groups caught the balls. They were selected to check Scott and the environment as well as to secure him in the cabinet.

When they mentioned tying him in the cabinet, my curiosity was challenged. I was unable to fathom what might be taking place in that room. I was excited about this night's adventure. I did not talk to anyone about the previous night for I wanted a unique experience with Scott. I went back to my room to prepare for the event.

We met thirty minutes before the séance in the hall outside the study. There were two lines formed, one for the women and the other for the men. Each student walked up and was patted down. A magnetic wand was used to check for metal. I walked over to a bowl and selected a number then entered the room which directed me to my seat.

This room had been used as a study by Gordon Higginson, a famous English medium. There, in front of the room, was

Chapter Nineteen: Adventures in the Cabinet

Gordon's medium's cabinet. This was just a wooden box with an opening to the front, top and bottom. There was a curtain on a rod in the front. The curtain was open and there was an armed chair inside. Outside of the cabinet was a small light with a red shade and a cd player. The ball catchers were checking the cabinet and room for trap doors, strings or anything else that could be used to create a false séance condition. There were other objects in the room; a ball, tambourine, bells and a trumpet.

I noticed that Scott was being checked by the ball catchers. They were patting him down before sitting him into the chair. They then pulled out of a bag some zip ties. They zip tied his hands and legs to the chair. They checked the chair again by pulling it to make sure it could not disconnect in any way. They then grabbed some scissors, cut the ties, and marked them. I was told this was so that if Scott tried to get out of the ties it would show that he did by moving the clamp. Marking would show that it was moved.

Soon after, all of us held hands as the lights went out. This was the darkest room I had ever experienced. A cd began to play and everyone started to sing. After about three songs, I felt the temperature drop in the room. There was a definite breeze amongst us. As our eyes adjusted to the darkness we saw a fog-like substance fill the room. I could see sparkles of light and a strange whitish grid above the room. I later found out it was called the matrix by many. This is a geometrically formed combination of lights and fog.

I heard a giggle of a small boy while we were singing. Then, people started saying they were being touched. I too was touched on the knee by a little hand. Then something pulled my hair. More giggling was heard all over the room as a ball came rolling into my feet. The music then stopped and someone welcomed Timmy. Timmy was a little boy from an English neighborhood. Timmy began beating a drum and shaking a tambourine. Then, he started talking to everyone in his childlike voice. I later learned Timmy was one of Scott's many guides. Timmy talked about Scott in third person. Timmy then wanted the group to sing again and the music began to play again.

Everyone started to sing including Timmy. The music then jumped tracks playing different songs. Someone asked Timmy if he didn't like the way we all sang. Timmy just giggled. As we sang, the bell rang and the trumpet began to soar through the air. A skeptic's first thought would be that someone was holding the trumpet, waving it. However, the ceilings in this room were over fifteen feet high. The trumpet soared high in the sky and would dive down at lengths far too long for anyone's arm to manipulate it. I sat there in awe with all the others admiring the work of Spirit.

Timmy settled down some as the music lowered. Timmy brought forth evidence of the spirit of someone to one of the audience members. He held conversations with many members of the audience. He then mentioned that we would have other visitors this night if we could keep the energy high. The music came alive and we all began to sing again. We were visited by an Indian chief who spoke of the ways of Spirit. We also experienced an experiment where the medium formed another voice box with the physical ectoplasm he produced. While doing this, we heard the medium's voice stretching. It was an odd sound but one I would not soon forget. The medium then brought through Frances Gum (Judy Garland) who sang *Over the Rainbow*. This was a bit odd at first but later made more sense. This was more than an imitation of someone attempting to sing like her. This was an experiment in getting the ectoplasm to form into that voice box. There could be no better way than to use the assistance from the spirit world of a great singer.

The séance continued for about two and a half hours. Towards the end, many of us felt something like a towel brushing over the tops of our heads. We then heard a loud crash. Muffled noises came from behind us and the red light was lit. There before our eyes, was Scott on the floor behind us lying outside the cabinet with the curtains all through his clothing still zip tied to the chair. His face was smashed to the ground. The thoughts ran rapid as we all looked in amazement. The cabinet had obviously flown over our heads and crashed about five feet behind us. Scott was tossed outside the cabinet with the curtains

Chapter Nineteen: Adventures in the Cabinet

all through his shirt while still connected to the cabinet. This would be virtually impossible with him being tied the way he was.

A few things were noted after the demonstration. Spirit uses the demonstration as an experiment. The experiment is different each time. No one knows what will happen but we all know that the energy of the situation has much to do with the phenomena that are created. Evidence is the key of every demonstration and is the most important portion of each session. A session without evidence is not considered a successful connection with the Spirit world. This was only my first experience with Scott and the evidence he can bring forth of the spirit world.

A subsequent journey across the pond brought me to an event with Scott and other mediums in Brighton. This event was dedicated to all of the physical mediums of the past. I was able to hear speeches from many of the retired physical mediums. I often wondered why many get out of the business. I was told that there are many health risks for physical mediums mostly from the production of ectoplasm. I began to understand why Spirit would allow this to happen. I knew someday that I would find that answer.

During this visit, I participated in a trance class with Glyn Edwards. Gordon Higginson's cabinet was in the class. Glyn placed me inside and I soon went into trance. After I was brought back to my awakened awareness, I was told by one of the instructors that I had overshadowed an Indian in full head gear. The head gear of feathers had also given off a bright gold hue. All the others in the group also validated the presence of that spirit.

Later that night during Scott's demonstration, we heard from Timmy as well as other visitors. The drum beat as it had the last time. This time there were two trumpets. In my amazement both trumpets flew up together simultaneously then split in midair flying to the outer reaches of the room. I noticed pin-like marks on the base of the trumpet where the luminous was. This was later explained to me as how ectoplasm holds onto the trumpets.

These lines were too small to be human fingers but I guess you could say they were the fingers of Spirit.

Another experiment done by Spirit, water was poured into glasses with precision. Although we could not see the act, we could hear it as well as one of Scott's guides was talking us through the experiment. I heard the snapping of each twist of the cap. I could hear the water pouring into the glass and the glass being placed back on the table.

During this session many of the old timers were present. The area was set as such. The chairs were two rows in horseshoe formation around the cabinet. The cabinet was backed to a stage. The stage was covered with chairs stacked so no one or nothing could get onto it. During the entire séance we all held hands. To end this session, we heard the voice of Spirit right in front of us. Then, in seconds, the lights were lifted upon a grunt from Scott. When the light came up, the cabinet was not only across the room but there were chairs stacked in perfect order around the cabinet. This time Scott was in the chair bound and again smashed face first on the floor. No curtains were in his clothes this time. This happened so fast the old timers jumped to their feet in amazement realizing that he had teleported from one location in the room to another.

The most recent event I attended took place in Wales. We were attending a workshop in an estate in the Brecon Beacon National Park. The estate was a beautiful castle set amongst rolling hills of green pastures. It was like stepping back in time. There were many familiar faces in the crowd. This time I had made the journey with some physical mediumship students from the center.

The séance at this location was similar like the previous ones. One difference is that many brought children's gifts to be donated post event to a charity for children. I purchased a small stuffed doll that was from a recent movie named, *Olaf*. There was a pre-séance lecture as before at which point we all turned in our gifts. The evening started as usual with everyone being searched. I had recently been to another medium's demonstration and knew the room would be hot. This time I dressed for the occasion. You

Chapter Nineteen: Adventures in the Cabinet

see in that area of the world I had learned from previous travels that they love heat. Even though it was freezing outside, the inside of the manor was unusually warm. The night before, everyone had left the séance drenched in sweat. This time I wore shorts and a t-shirt.

After being searched, I entered the room to find that I was lucky enough to have been seated directly in front of the cabinet. Between me and the cabinet on the floor space was a small, lit Christmas tree and all the gifts were around the tree. The usual trumpet, drum, tambourine and other musical instruments were present. The chairs were all lined around the room. The temperature was what felt like over ninety degrees. There were approximately seventy people in the room.

While we were singing some English tunes, we saw the lights on the Christmas tree blink on and off. They then went off and we heard the unwrapping of presents and what sounded like several children laughing and playing. I heard a child's voice call out the name of the doll I had donated. Then, the child's voice thanked me for the gift. We continued to sing as Timmy visited again. There were a couple validations of Spirit presence to some of the audience members through touch. The trumpet once again began to fly around the room.

At this time periodically the red light lamp would come on. You could see Scott tied to the chair but some rod looking substance kept opening the curtain from below so I could see Scott in his chair. It appeared the rod was formed from his navel and that it was moving the curtain. The lights went off as we continued to sing. Another of Scott's guides came through telling us of mediumship in the old days. There was mention of many of the mediums who had passed. Soon after, the séance ended with Scott still in the cabinet but the curtains were wrapped all around him.

*****

Séance is an experiment with Spirit. All the conditions should be set forth to create a secure, safe and evidential sitting.

Only what Spirit selects will be produced. There is no set agenda. Spirit is using the environment to create what it can with the energy that is created in the room. Any medium that can honestly tell what is going to happen during their séance is probably not working with Spirit. Scott thus far has been the most genuine physical medium demonstrator that I have met. My journey and research will continue until I transfer into the next life. This is because Spirit has no limits. We at times prevent ourselves from allowing Spirit to manifest the evidential phenomena that makes this type of mediumship so unique.

Chapter Twenty
The Power of Spirit

Our relationship with Spirit is just like any other relationship we have in this world. If you cultivate it, it grows and strengthens, if you neglect it, it dissipates. With each new encounter in the séance room, we find that Spirit is taking us to new levels. We also notice that Spirit's ability to manipulate the physical is strengthening as well.

As much as I am amazed by channeling and other forms of trance mediumship, I still love doing table work. It is one thing for Spirit to manipulate energy in a meter or other electronic device, but for Spirit to have the power to lift a hundred pound table as if it was feather, continues to amaze me.

Sid shared one of his most powerful experiences during a table tipping session:

On a hot, humid evening in Central Florida in the town of Cassadaga, family and friends gathered for yet another séance. The temperature outside was well in the 80s. The air was thick with moisture as we all entered the medium's house. The unique part about this home is that in the back of the kitchen is a doorway. The doorway leads down into a cellar which is used as the séance room.

The room has an area where the table is located used in the séance. The table is a wooden table that weighs at least eighty pounds and has eight chairs around it. The other side houses a medium's cabinet. There are smaller tables along the back wall. Pictures and memoirs are located on the walls from people who have passed onto the other side. There are trumpets like those used in séances hanging from the ceiling and luminous paint in areas so that there is some light during the séance. There is also a presence of Indian cultural objects in the room.

The usual opening prayers and songs were sung into the night causing the table to react. The first action of the table was a loud knock in the center of the table. The table then began to glide as we were singing old songs. The table gave messages to most of us there sitting at the table. This is done by asking a question and if the table reacts then the answer is yes and if the table doesn't react it is no. I enjoyed a time with the lady who raised me while my mother worked. The table slid up to me and gave me the best hug. The table will caress you on the abdomen and is known as a hug.

One of the guests who had been suffering from stomach issues received a healing. The table stood up on two legs and walked over to the guest named Rick. The other side of the table faced Daphne. The temperature changes in the room were noted. The area facing Rick was warm and the area facing Daphne was cold. The energy was being pulled from Daphne and those that surrounded her and was being transferred to Rick.

During the healing phase, the table would not move. The medium asked for Daphne and the others to try to push the table down off its two legs. All tried to push it over but were unsuccessful. The table stood at attention for about twenty minutes before it gently came down on its own thus signifying that the healing was completed. When the table reached the floor completely, it gently slid to the center of the group and just stopped.

Singing began and soon the table started to move again. The table slid its way over to Deidra and began rubbing her tummy. Deidra asked, "Mom is that you?" The table began to buck like a wild bronco. Deidra's face lit up with excitement as she shared fond memories with her mother. The table slid to me and my spouse to give hugs and then went to my other sister Sandra. They were all sharing moments with our mom filling the room with happiness and joy.

Chapter Twenty: The Power of Spirit

Suddenly, Sandra yelled, "Mom, do you remember how you used to do cart wheels?"

At that instance the table flipped up on its side and began to roll around the room. You could hear the excitement in everyone's voice as they cheered my mother on. The table went round and round doing cart wheel after cart wheel. Tears of amazement and joy came to most eyes this night.

The table flipped back up and for a short moment literally creaked, "goodbye" and became still.

Undeniably, Sid's mother's manipulation of the table had changed from the first time he and his family visited a table tipping session.

One of the biggest questions for me was whether Spirit was really moving the table or are we, the mediums, raising the energy so much that we are psychically causing it to move? Even though I do believe in physical phenomena, it was a question worth asking.

Sid has always stood by his opinion that it was both Spirit and the mediums energy creating the movement. This might explain why there was a lot more phenomena producing in Cassadaga where a séance room had been operating for years, as opposed to our séance room which was only a bit over a year old. We had already established that when we held sessions with the table in which all of the participants were mediums, the energy was more prevalent. In mental mediumship, it is constantly being pointed out where a medium slips into more of a psychic mode rather than connected to Spirit. Could this not happen with physical phenomena as well? I wanted proof but did not lose sleep over trying to find it. Then one evening, my question was answered when I least expected it.

One early Sunday evening, Silvia and I met for circle at the center. Sid was meeting with several other people as they worked on a play that was largely based on our experiences with Stephanie in the séance room. While his group read over the preliminary script, Silvia and I decided to sit in the power for a while with no specific intentions, except to see what was presented to us. Neither of us touched the table. We merely sat at it, with our hands on our laps, open palm, facing upwards.

Silvia turned on some meditation music. It was not anything too hypnotic as to put us in trance, just a nice mellow piano piece with sound effects of nature interlaced in it. Suddenly, we heard the table creak as if it moved. At first, we both ignored it because neither of us touched it with any intent therefore, by what we had always experienced, the table should not move. Several seconds later, we heard it creak again. This time, we opened our eyes. The table was vibrating. We both looked at each other and lightly placed our hands atop of it. As soon as we touched it, it jumped all over the place and pushed hard against me.

"Stephanie, is that you?" I asked.

The table jumped around wildly with excitement. Silvia and I asked her questions but she continued to jump erratically. Then I realized why she was so excited.

I asked her, "Stephanie, are you excited because Sid is doing a play about you?"

The table danced and jumped up and down faster and faster. Soon the table was rising up off of the floor completely, and crashing back down into the floor. The more I asked her about the play, the wilder it became. So she had the table lifting up and slamming into the floor with loud thuds.

I said, "Stephanie, I see what you are trying to do. You want Sid to hear you so he comes in here. Is that right?"

The table responded this time with short jumps.

Without even giving it any thought as to what she might do, I then told her, "Well, if you want him, you will have to go get him. So go on."

Without hesitation, the table literally levitated completely off of the floor and flew across the room. It crashed into the door. By now it had left both of our hands and was moving completely on its own. We both witnessed as the table hit the door then backed up, hitting it again several times. Each time it did, it sounded as if it was going to crash through to the other side.

Chapter Twenty: The Power of Spirit

Finally the noise caught Sid's attention. He attempted to open the door but as he opened it, the table hit the door again, blocking his entry.

He called out, "Stephanie, if you want me to come in, you have to move the table."

Even though he was not present in the room with us, he knew she was controlling the table. The table gently moved back several feet to allow him to enter the room. It then crashed against him. He asked her to calm down so we could find out what it was she was trying to express. Through various yes/no questions, we were able to understand that she was very excited about a play being written in her honor. As it turned out, during the meeting of those involved, there had been some concern over to whether or not use her real name or a variation of it, or to use something completely different. It seemed that she wanted Sid to know that she wanted her name used as her character. After Sid promised to make the change in the name and promised to keep her directly involved in the production, the table quietly stopped moving and we bid Stephanie farewell.

It was a shock to all of us that the table had moved the way it did. We examined the table after the incident and saw tiny nicks in it where the edges had been chipped off and paint markings from the door not just in one place but all around the edges of the table. Not only was the table levitating up off of the floor and literally flying into the door, but each time it backed up and slammed again, it was also turning like a wheel. We all knew that the table did not have the chips or paint marks prior to that day's incident. The table in our séance room seats eight people and is between a hundred and two hundred pounds. Not one of us could lift it let alone move it the way it did that day.

Not only was my question answered, it was answered without my seeking the answer from my daughter. She knew my mind, though. She read my thoughts. She knew that I desired to have an answer so that I would know without doubt that it is Spirit that makes the table move in the séance. She also proved that our loved ones not only can and do communicate through a variety of methods but they also are aware of things going on around us.

They are still a part of our lives, even if we are not always aware of it. This knowledge, this validation that gave to me that day, strengthened my belief in the power of Spirit. She showed me just how far Spirit will go when we sit back and allow the power to take control without expectations or limitations being placed.

Chapter Twenty-One
Final Thoughts

I stepped into this arena in order to better communicate with my daughter. She urged me, in my first session with Sid, to move forward on my spiritual quest. She told Sid that the more I moved forward, the closer she would get to me. That was the point of this journey. She held up her end of this agreement. The assessments I got from the mentoring mediums offered just the advice I needed to further propel me on my path and my connection to my daughter. It also helped me help others who needed to heal from the loss of a loved one. The point is to facilitate healing and to help others on the same journey to heal.

Having had the experiences I did over the past several years, as much as I still regret that my daughter is not here physically, I believe that her work in this world had come to completion. She continues to work in my life and in others' by bringing healing messages from the other side. She continues, in the afterlife, to make other people smile, laugh, think, and heal. To this day, everyone she touches, she leaves them with a gift.

During one of her sessions, she announced to me, at a mental séance, that I needed to complete unfinished projects that had fallen by the wayside. She also told me that someone connected with the media would be contacting me. Shortly after that, someone did contact me but it was to tell me that Stephanie had appeared to her during her meditations. Even though she did not know Stephanie during her life, she had met her during a physical séance and recognized her energy. She had also seen photographs of her so she knew what she looked like during her life. This woman works in media. Who knows what might become of this alliance, perhaps another gift from Spirit.

My own journey is not over. My daughter's original message urged me to share what I knew with the world. I did not want to disappoint her. The more I experience, the more I see, the more I learn about our connection to Spirit. What I believed twenty years ago is vastly different from what I know now. I hope to continue on this journey learning something new, evolving every step of the way.

We continue to sit in our mediumship circle in the séance room and conduct our experiments. Stephanie, Laura, and the others come and discuss what the afterlife is like. The Shaman instructs us on what we can do as a group and as individuals to grow spiritually.

As we grow in our relationship to Spirit, we are allowed to experience a deeper connection to the other side. Where we once only felt their presence coming in through the portal, we now have begun to actually see the faces of these spirits floating in the ectoplasm and hovering over the mediums as if they are waiting in line to have their turn to speak to us.

The messages we receive are more concise and are easily validated. Silvia finally had the opportunity to be the sitter in a channeling session and see her father overshadow another medium. Desperate to hear him speak, she begged for him to talk through the medium. The medium was a novice, no words came forth. I connected mentally to him and he showed me a bridal hairpiece with tiny seashells in it. I described to Silvia the vision. After the session, she showed me a photograph on her phone of her father. It was the same face I saw overshadowing the new medium. She then flipped to another photograph of her mother as a young bride. Her veil was covered in tiny embroidered sea shells. Her family on the other side continued to visit during sessions as her wedding approached. She knew they were there with her. She knew that her father was proud and would accompany her down the aisle.

Every encounter brings us to a better understanding of why we are here and where we are going when we leave this existence.

Chapter Twenty-One: Final Thoughts

Sid said:

This is a growing process, for everyone, including Spirit. We are learning how this works together, to become this union, this oneness, which is what we think the universe really is. The more I do, the better it gets.

The goal is that no matter where you are in your life, to become part of the oneness in this universe. We are all a 360 degree ball, like a snow globe. Every particle, the earth, the stars, plants, animals, and all of us are connected. We are all in the oneness. The heart is the main chakra. You must always keep it open and keep nourishing it.

Stephanie basically said the same thing:

You can see God too; all you have to do is look in the mirror. He's in there. He's in all of us.

Every day we encounter new experiences in our relationships with Spirit. As much as this becomes a way of life for many of us, we all need to remember to spend some time, simply experiencing and enjoying this lifetime that we have. Our loved ones on the other side do not expect nor desire for us to spend every waking hour obsessing over communicating with them or others on the other side. Everything in life, including mediumship requires balance. It is easy for someone who is grieving the loss of a loved one to become obsessed with connecting to that person all the time. Part of the journey is knowing that our connection to those we love cannot be severed, even by death. We have to balance our lives with our relationships with those we have in this world too. The medium's job is not only to prove that life exists beyond death but to help those who are mourning to heal and continue to live out their lives to their fullest capacity. Our journey continues on in this world and will pick up where it left off with those on the other side when it is our time to join them.

Since this writing of this book, Sid and I have expanded into other cities to deliver messages of hope and offer guidance to those who seek to walk this path. We are continually looking for new ways to expand our knowledge and push Spirit to new levels of communicating with us.

The accounts that we have documented herein actually took place. The visions, the messages, and the experiences that Spirit brought to us were validated by others present. We know beyond all doubt that what we saw, heard, and felt were real. Every experience validated the one before it giving way to the next. The final message from Spirit was all along and continues to be... *Believe!*

Glossary

Altered State of Consciousness (ASC)

A term used to refer to any state of consciousness that is different from "normal" states of waking or sleeping. ASCs include hypnosis, trance, ecstasy, psychedelic and meditative experience. ASCs do not necessarily have paranormal features.

Apparition

The visual appearance of an entity whose physical body is not present. Generally, an apparition applies to any form of entity where it is distinguishable as a person or animal. The apparition can appear in partial or full-bodied.

Apport / Asport

An apport is a solid object that seemingly appears from nowhere in the presence of a medium. Asport is any object the 'spirits' or medium makes disappear or teleports to another location.

Astral body

The body a person seems to occupy during an out-of-body experience.

Astral Plane

A world that exists above the physical world.

Astral projection

An out-of-body experience (OBE).

Astrology

A theory and practice which attempts to identify the ways in which astronomical events are correlated with events on earth.

Aura

An energy field that some psychics see surrounding the living body.

Automatic Writing
Writing without being aware of the contents, as when a medium apparently transcribes written messages from disembodied spirits.

Bilocation
Being (or appearing to be) in two different places at the same time.

Card Guessing
An experimental tests for ESP in which subjects guess the identity of a set of cards.

Cerebral Anoxia
Lack of oxygen to the brain, often causing sensory distortions and hallucinations. Sometimes used to explain features of the Near Death Experience.

Chakra
An energy center in the human body.

Channeling
The process by which a medium allows a spirit to communicate through his or her person.

Clairaudience
Auditory form of ESP (compare with Clairvoyance).

Claircognizance
The ability to know something without a physical explanation as to why.

Clairessence
Using the sense of smell to obtain information.

Clairgustance
Using tastes to obtain information.

Clairsentience
Physical sensations form of ESP.

Clairvoyance
A subset of ESP. The viewing of distant scenes not apparent to the eye, may appear externally - either replacing the normal

Glossary

visual scene (visions) or being incorporated into it (as could be the case with apparitions) - or internally, in the form of mental imagery and intuition.

Cold Reading

A technique using a series of general statements, questions, and answers that allows fake mediums, mind-readers, and magicians to obtain previously unknown information about a person. (Reader has no prior knowledge).

Collective Apparition

An unusual type of 'ghost' sighting in which more than one person sees the same phenomenon.

Control

In experimental parapsychology a procedure undertaken in order to ensure that the experiment is conducted in a standard fashion and so that results are not unduly influenced by extraneous factors.

Crisis Apparition

An apparition that is seen when the subject is at the point of death or if the victim of a serious illness or injury; often the spirit of someone returning to say goodbye or let loved ones know that he/she is ok.

Curse

To speak a wish of evil against someone or call down forces to hurt someone.

Demon

An evil spirit that was never human.

Discarnate

Earthbound spirits that exist without a physical body.

Doorkeeper

Also called Gatekeeper, is a spirit who opens the doors of communication between a medium and spirits.

Ectoplasm

A substance, which emanates from the body of a medium during a trance. This often appears as a mist-like substance.

Electromagnetic Field
A field propagated by a combination of electric and magnetic energy, which radiates from radio and light waves to gamma and cosmic rays. It is believed that when spirits manifest, they create an electromagnetic field.

EMF Detector
An instrument that measures electromagnetic energy. Also known as a Gauss Meter or magnetometer.

ESP
ESP or extrasensory perception is considered what scientists refer to as a receptive psi. This type of experience usually involves the transfer of information.

EVP
Electronic voice phenomena. Voices captured on audiotape when no one is present. It is believed that these voices are from spirits attempting to communicate with living people.

Evoking
The act of calling forth a specific spirit; whether it be lower vibrational non-human entities or earthbound human ones.

Experiment
A test carried out under controlled conditions.

Experimental Group
A group of subjects who undergo a specific experimental procedure. Often results from this group are compared with those of a control group.

Experimental Parapsychology
Parapsychology research involving experimental methods rather than survey techniques or the investigation of spontaneous cases.

Experimenter
The person who conducts the experiment.

Experimenter Effect
Influence that the experimenter's personality or behavior may have on the results of an experiment.

Glossary

False Awakening
An experience in which a person believes he or she has woken up, but actually is still dreaming.

Gallery (Platform Work)
A group of people who gather to receive messages from a mental medium who is reading for the entire group.

Gatekeeper
See Doorkeeper

Ghost
A form of apparition, usually the visual appearance of a deceased human's 'spirit soul' or that of a crisis apparition.

Ghost Hunt / Ghost Investigation
A ghost hunt is an informal attempt to simply sight or record a 'ghost' in a location similar to others known to be haunted. A ghost investigation, on the other hand, is a carefully controlled research project, set up to record paranormal activity, usually at a location known, or presumed to be haunted.

Hallucination
Perception of sights, sounds, etc., that is not actually present. Ghosts, as we define them, are not hallucinations, because they have a real, external cause.

Haunting
Recurrent sounds of human activity, sightings of apparitions, and other psychic phenomena, in a location when no one is there physically.

Hypnosis
State like sleep in which the subject acts only on external suggestion.

Illusion
A distorted perception of objects or events causing a discrepancy between what is perceived and what is reality.
Intuition
The non-paranormal ability to grasp the elements of a situation or to draw conclusions about complex events in ways that go beyond a purely rational or intellectual analysis.
Invoking
The act of calling up (conjuring) a spirit to walk-in or possess yourself or another person.

Kirlian photography
A photographic method involving high frequency electric current, discovered by S.D. & V. Kirlian in the Soviet Union. Kirlian photographs often show colored halos or "auras" surrounding objects.

Laying on of Hands
A process by which certain healers profess to be able to heal patients by touch.
Levitation
The lifting of physical objects by psychokinesis (PK).
Life Review
Flashback memories of the whole of a person's life often associated with the near-death experience.
Longbody
A web of living connections among people, places, and objects.
Lucid Dreaming
Dreaming in which the person is aware that the experience is a dream. Often associated with feelings of aliveness and freedom, and with the ability to control dream events.

Glossary

Materialization
The deliberate, usually temporary, visible and/or physical formation of a spirit.

Medical Intuitive
A psychic who can detect illness in the physical body without physical means.

Medium
A psychic through who spirits can communicate. A medium can be either a mental or physical medium.

Medium (direct voice)
A trance medium that apparently acts as a transmitter for the voices of disembodied spirits.

Medium (materialization)
A physical medium that seems to be able to give physical form to the deceased from a substance called "ectoplasm".

Metaphysics
Derived from the Latin word "meta" which means "beyond," metaphysics would literally mean that which is beyond the laws of physics. The study of psychical research.

NDE
Near death experience. Experienced when the person is in fact clinically dead for a period of time. The person usually feels himself or herself leaving their body and sometimes observing the location and people around them, they usually often view their own lifeless bodies, then the person feels as though they are rising up through some sort of tunnel towards a bright light. Sometimes they may see or hear a deceased family member or friend, or even a religious figure of some kind. The person having this experience is usually told it is not the right time, or they decide themselves it is not time to die, and they return to their bodies.

OBE
Out of body experience, or astral projection. This is the sensation or experience many people have of actually leaving their body for a period of time, this is where the spirit or soul leaves the body. This can also be described as "traveling clairvoyance."

Orb
A sphere of electromagnetic energy produced by spirits. Also called a globule.

Ouija Board
Game board manufactured by the Parker Brothers Company. Used to communicate with spirits. Some believe this "communication" is caused by the collective unconscious of the participants.

Paranormal
Occurrences that take place outside the natural order of things. This would include ghosts, UFO's, ESP and other things difficult to explain by nature but in the realm of the natural.

Parapsychology
The branch of science that studies psychic phenomena.

Photoplasm
A term used by some to describe a source of energy that can be seen by the eye and has the ability to function the same way ectoplasm does, i.e.; moving objects and creating apparitions.

Planchette
from the French for "little plank", is a small, usually heart-shaped flat piece of wood equipped with two wheeled castors and a pencil-holding aperture, used to facilitate automatic writing. The use of planchettes to produce mysterious written messages gave rise to the belief that the devices foster communication with spirits as a form of mediumship.

Poltergeist
A German word meaning 'noisy or rowdy ghost'.

Glossary

PK - Psychokinesis
The power of the mind to affect matter without physical contact.

Precognition
The ability to predict things beyond present knowledge.

Psi
A letter in the Greek alphabet that denotes psychic phenomena.

Psyche
The Greek word for "self", "mind", or "soul".

Psychic
A person with above average ESP abilities.

Psychic Healing
A mode of healing affected by the psychic abilities of the healer.

Psychic Surgery
The supposed ability to paranormally perform invasive surgery using no conventional medical tools.

Psychometry
ESP of events associated with inanimate objects.

Remote Viewing
(1) Another term for clairvoyance.
(2) An ESP procedure in which a percipient attempts to become aware psychically of the experience of an agent who is at a distant, unknown target location.

Repressed Psychokinetic Energy
A theoretical psychic force produced, usually unconsciously, by an individual undergoing physical or mental trauma. When released, the power causes paranormal occurrences such as poltergeist activity.

Retrocognition
The awareness of objects and events that existed in a past time RSPK - Recurrent spontaneous psychokinesis. A possible cause of apparent poltergeist activity.

Sceptic (skeptic)

A person inclined to discount the reality of the paranormal and to be critical of parapsychological research. Generally seeks rational or scientific explanations for the phenomenon studied by parapsychologists.

Scrying

A term used to cover a wide range of divination techniques which parapsychology would tend to classify as types of ESP. Most scrying techniques involve some degree of fixation on a surface with a clear optical depth or on an area, which shows random patterns, the idea being that subconscious information available to the scrying will be manifested in their interpretation of the imagery or random patterns they see.

Séance

A group of people who gather in an effort to communicate with the dead.

Sensitive

A person with psychic abilities.

Shadow Ghost

A black, mist like spirit that has no discernable features. It is usually demonic in nature and is sometimes described by witnesses as a "black shape".

Shaman

A 'wizard' in tribal societies who is an intermediary between the living, the dead, and the gods.

Sitter

Client who is receiving messages from loved ones through a medium.

Spirit Photography

A spirit photograph captures the image of a ghost on film. Many of these are supposedly intended as a mere portrait of a living human being, but when the film is developed, an ethereal ghostly face or figure can be seen hovering near the subject. This may also incorporate orbs, vortexes, and mists to some degree.

Spiritualism

A belief system that 'spirits' of the dead can (and do) communicate with living humans in the material world.

Glossary

Subjective Apparitions
Apparitions or phenomena that are hallucinations created by our minds.

Stigmata
Unexplained markings on a person's body that correspond to the wounds of Christ.

Supernatural
Something that exists or occurs through some means other than any known force in nature. As opposed to paranormal, the term 'supernatural' often connotes divine or demonic intervention.

Table Tipping
A type of physical séance in which a table is used as the conductor for spirit communication; spirits use the table to answer questions for loved ones.

Telekinesis
Paranormal movement of objects.

Telepathy
The direct passing of information from one mind to another.

Teleportation
A kind of paranormal transportation in which an object is moved from one distinct location to another, often through a solid object such as a wall.

Thought Form
An apparition produced by the power of the human mind.

Trance
A sleeplike state in which there is a change of consciousness.

Vortex (Vortices, pl)
(1) A photographed anomaly that appears as a funnel that is not seen at the time of the photograph that presumably represents the third phase of physical manifestation of a spirit in photographs.

(2) A whirling mass of energy in the earth. Vortices can be positive (releasing energy) or negative (pulling energy).

White Noise

A hiss-like sound, formed by compiling all audible frequencies.

Discover other fine publications at:

http://www.darkoakpress.com

www.ingramcontent.com/pod-product-compliance
Lightning Source LLC
LaVergne TN
LVHW011417080426
835512LV00005B/113